# FILL

# IN THE

# BLANK

Ten Strangers and Their
Untiring Quest to Appear
on Wheel of Fortune

A Laurel Book

Laurel Publishing House

LPHBOOKS.COM

Ordering Information: Quantity sales – Special discounts are available on quantity purchases by corporations, associations, religious organizations, and other charities. For more details, contact publisher at the web Site above.

ISBN: 978-0-9985280-0-7

Library of Congress Control Number: 2017910742

Printed in the United States of America
Published simultaneously in Canada

January 2017 – First Edition
17 16 15 14 13 / 10 9 8 7 6 5 4 3 2 1

# PRAISE FOR FILL IN THE BLANK

*For the first time in documented literary history, a singular book has won National Awards in both Games and Religion categories.*

Best Book in the Category of Games and Puzzles

Award-Winning Finalist in Religion: Christianity

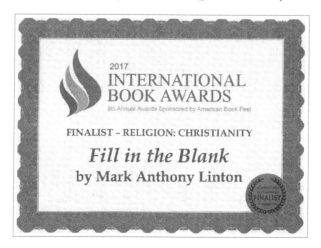

"A rollicking ride and a fantastic story that explores the power of dreams, friendship, and faith, Fill in the Blank by Mark Anthony Linton is a thrilling story that is every bit as entertaining as it is empowering. Mark has been a huge fan of the wheel and now his eyes are set on Culver City. But luck doesn't seem to come his way. He's failed twice to become a contestant on the Emmy-winning show, and is poised for the third chance, hoping against all hope that things turn out better this time around. Watch his adventure as he encounters strangers who become friends and some who succeed in becoming contestants, winning a fortune on America's favorite game show.

"THE BOOK READS LIKE A SHOW. A MASTERPIECE IN ENTERTAINMENT, A PAGE-TURNER WITH A FAST-PACED PLOT AND EXCITING CHARACTERS."

Mark Anthony Linton takes readers on an exciting journey to uncover the thrill behind Wheel of Fortune, showing readers what it takes to get on board. Creating a compelling cast of characters that readers will fall for, this author crafts a tale that combines humor with soul-searching messages to take them on an adventure that will stir the noblest of sentiments and emotions in their hearts. The book reads like a show. As I turned page after page, I kept focused on what would become of the protagonist, watching his every move and wondering if he would succeed in achieving his lifelong dream. Fill in the Blank is a masterpiece in entertainment, a page-turner with a fast-paced plot and exciting characters." - *Five Star Review from Readers' Favorite*

According to Wheel of Fortune's website:
"Last year over a million people requested the
chance to audition for Wheel of Fortune. Fewer
than 600 were selected to appear on the show."
(0.0006 percent). Those aren't the best odds.

---

"Some people are waiting for you to fail.
I say, make 'em wait!" *Mark Anthony Linton*

_ _ L _ * _ _ * _ _ _ T _
N _ T * _ _ * S _ _ _ T

Category: Phrase

Get inspired by a group of strangers who met on social media, created a lighthearted gathering without a set agenda, and 50% (5 of 10) became contestants on America's favorite game-show, winning over two-hundred thousand dollars.

―――――――――

"Some people are cheering for you to succeed. I say, make 'em proud!" *Mark Anthony Linton*

# WALK * BY * FAITH
# NOT * BY * SIGHT

2 Corinthians 5:7

# Contents

IN MEMORY of
EILEEN "*Chip*" VAN KIRK

*Chip was proud of her only son –Kyle M. Buckles*
*Communications Director, U.S. House of Representatives*
*and dearly loved her husband –Sergeant Bruce Van Kirk*
*who retired after serving 25 years in the U.S. Marines*
*and appeared on Wheel of Fortune Salutes our Military.*

*We met every day at 1pm, yet we have never met.*
*I like to believe our love for Wheel of Fortune*
*in some way, brought us together.*
*The quality of our friendship, in so many ways*
*could only have been Heaven sent.*

# Thank **YOU**

Wheel of Fortune winners ::: Steven Chai, David Rigsby, Emilbert de Leon & Chad Mosher. I BLAME ALL of you for prolonging my miseries with your constant encouragement and support.

Short bus Crew members ::: Eric Pierce, Kim Doyle Wille, Jesse & Susie Bush, Rebecca Stead & 'Chip' Van Kirk for sharing their afternoons with me. They are the heart and soul of this book.

Shae Sterling ::: my listener, my faith builder, my developmental editor behind the scenes, who was going to help give birth to this *best-selling autobiographical novel*, and we did it.

Somica Nation ::: my beautiful mother, who had the arduous task of raising four incorrigible boys by herself in a foreign country. She prayed for us when we did not know to pray. Not a day goes by that I am not grateful for that. I love you, mama.

To all the devoted ::: friends, Facebook friends, Twitter followers, former childhood friends, colleagues, and family members who never stopped asking, "When are you going to get on that show?"

Here's the story... now please, just leave me alone.

# FILL IN THE BLANK

*Ten Strangers and Their Untiring*

*Quest to Appear on Wheel of Fortune*

Award-Winning Autobiographical Novel

*by*

# Mark Anthony Linton

"Take the first step in faith. You don't have to see the whole staircase, just take the first step."
– Dr. Martin Luther King, Jr.

WHAT DOES THAT MEAN? When presented with a challenge, do you find yourself reluctant to start until you gather more information?

Dr. King's quote emphasizes the importance of faith. Despite the situation, King challenges us to take the initial step, believing that the remainder of the staircase exists.

In life, there are few guarantees, and we need to approach it one day at a time. Every journey begins with a single step, and that step is taken in faith, believing the staircase will become visible over time. When you have faith, you know something is real, even if you cannot see or touch it right away.

If you don't have faith that the first step will lead to an entire staircase, then you could fail to make this important step, and miss out on a life changing opportunity.

WHY IS FAITH IMPORTANT? It is important because it demonstrates our willingness to trust God, though outcome isn't immediately visible.

Consider faith a verb, an action of the heart, as it requires one to trust when there's no guarantee. This expression of hope, otherwise known as faith, is important because it honors God, and God always honors faith.

Some view the exercise of faith as a very daunting task, when in reality it's the opposite. God does not require this grand gesture, instead he says if we have faith the size of a mustard seed, we can move mountains.

If you have ever seen a mustard seed, then you know that it's extremely small, less than 2 millimeters in diameter. The mustard seed is a reminder that with the smallest bit of faith, nothing is impossible. We just need to show confidence in God, His promises, and His ability to move in any situation.

I believe that faith is knowing for certain that a step really does exists, even if the top of the staircase seems invisible to our eyes. The staircase is a flexible metaphor, as the step and staircase apply to any avenue in life.

A romantic relationship might be one of the staircases you begin climbing. Maybe it was the nostalgia of aging that made me "*Google*" my childhood sweetheart on New Year's Eve. That was the first step.

I unknowingly entered my information into a networking site. You know the site (mylife.com) that tells you when someone is searching for you. She received the following:

"A 42 year old man who lives in Atlanta, Georgia and attended the University of Maryland College Park is looking for you..." Little did I know that what I was searching for, was also searching for me.

I received a *Facebook* inbox message the following day; "Happy New Year Mark! It has definitely been a long time. While I do not recall registering for MyLife, I received an email stating you searched for me? On a really rough day, it brought about a smile." We reunited on Valentine's Day in Baltimore. That was the second step.

As we continue climbing the staircase, faith is knowing for certain that the other person is as interested and as committed in getting to the top of the stairs as you are.

It could be a transition from employee to entrepreneur. The biggest skill needed to change your mind-set from employee to entrepreneur is faith.

Unlike a job where you believe that if you work so many hours, or at least show up, that a company will pay you a certain wage for that time, being an entrepreneur requires you to have faith that if you provide value, then you will be paid.

Having faith, you know your work will solve the problems of your audience. Having faith, believing that if you put in the effort today, it will turn into income down the road. Having faith, you know that your labor is not in vain, and the effort invested will produce fruit.

As I am writing this *best-selling autobiographical novel*, I trust, I have faith, that I am providing a value to you. I believe that many will read, many will receive, the Spirit will be felt, and faith will be strengthened. That is a promise that I leave with you. I live in faith, not in fear.

Joseph Campbell, author of one of the most influential books of the 20th Century – *The Hero with a Thousand Faces* once famously wrote: "The cave you fear to enter holds the treasure that you seek."

WHERE CAN I APPLY THIS IN MY LIFE? Dr. King's quote is the story of my life and the basis for this book.

Five years ago, I noticed a lump under the skin of my forehead, just above my right eye. It grew from the size of a lentil to the size of a marble. It could be pushed around beneath the skin. I tried pressing it down to eliminate it and once hit it with a heavy book, but it still remained.

I arranged to have a diagnosis. The doctor recommended a computed tomography (CT) scan. The results showed a tumor.

When you are diagnosed with a tumor, there's an instant response emotionally, mentally, and physically. Terror was my first reaction to the word "*tumor.*"

I was referred to a specialist who biopsied the tumor. The examination found the mass to be (benign), meaning it was non-cancerous. It is similar to cancer because the growth is a result of abnormal cells.

However, unlike cancer, it is unable to spread to other parts of the body. Because there were some neoplastic cells contained within the tumor, it was recommended that I get a CT scan every year for the next 5 years.

Surgery was the next step and the location of the tumor posed the next threat. My surgeon assured me that 299 of 300 patient surgeries per year to remove non-cancerous (benign) tumors end in success.

I reminded him that he would be cutting into the front of my head, commonly known as my face. I like my face.

Fast forward 5 years to September, I just resigned as a (Real-Estate-Career-Manager) with *Better Homes and Gardens* in Atlanta and can go back to wearing hats all day long.

It's fitting that September is dubbed National Hat Month. I've over 30 hats in my wardrobe.

Many of us only have fashion in mind when we purchase head-toppers. 5 years, still afraid to undergo surgery to remove tumor, I wore hats religiously to hide the lump that continued to grow in the middle of my face. Hats acted as a security blanket; it's something I could hide behind.

The first day after my last day in Corporate America, I began thinking of jobs I could wear a hat – baseball player, construction worker, limousine driver, pilot, policeman, rabbi, author (maybe), any one of the *Village People*.

I marched into my closet on a mission to find the perfect hat for my first day as a (Real-Estate-Bird-Dog), someone who tries to locate properties with substantial investment potential with the intent to repair or remodel and sell for a sizable profit. The term itself is a reference to hunting dogs that would point to the location of birds and then retrieve them once the hunter had shot them.

I have taken a Real Estate career path, from a manager to a dog, governed by the philosophy – "I have to wear a hat," instead of taking a career path based on what I actually wanted to do with my life, in spite of my anxiety about the tumor on my forehead.

I spotted a navy blue Atlanta Braves embroidered hat. As I reached up to grab it, I felt a sharp pain in my neck. I started to feel dizzy. I could feel the right side of my body going numb. The feeling is akin to when your legs go to sleep. In that single, pure moment, God spoke to me, and it was undeniable:

---

*"Walk in holiness before me now, do not look back, fear not what will happen, for I will provide, and I will provide beyond your wildest dreams, be strong, and be courageous, and do it."*

When God tells you to do something, you do it! Even if you do it with your knees shaking. I immediately placed a call to my Doctor. I had finally developed enough Faith to have surgery. I fully trusted Him – *unconditionally*, no matter what.

During procedure under local anesthesia, I was awake, but felt no pain, the tumor was excised then examined.

I snapped the obligatory post-surgery selfie for *Facebook* with Dr. Hodson, then gave myself a hard look in the mirror. 12 stitches did not look so bad, after all. I high-5'd everyone for being so helpful and thanked God for being so faithful.

As I headed towards the exit, I had a beautiful experience with the Holy Spirit. "Three Little Birds" by *Bob Marley* started playing on PA system. God spoke to me through a reggae song. I did not see him physically in front of me. I did not hear his voice directly, but I had faith it was him.

God speaks to us in a host of ways which we must be careful not to miss. I recall a story in Old Testament where God spoke through a donkey (Numbers 22:28-30). Some might say a donkey sounds better than me. That didn't stop me from Singing'

*Rise up this morning*
*smiled with the rising sun.*
*Three little birds*
*pitch by my doorstep.*
*Singing sweet songs*
*of melodies pure and true.*
*Saying, this is my message to you-ou-ou.*

---

*Singing: Don't worry 'bout a thing.*
*'Cause every little thing gonna be alright.*
*Singing: Don't worry 'bout a thing.*
*'Cause every little thing gonna be alright.*

While Dr. King's quote was not on my mind at the time, it certainly did apply. I knew there was the first stair. I knew there were stairs going up the staircase. I still cannot see more than a step or two ahead, but I have blind faith that the stairs are there. My latest (CT) scans were clean – I AM STILL CANCER FREE!

---

"Someone, somewhere is praying for that very thing you take for granted." *Mark Anthony Linton*

I Sat Down with Ten Strangers for
Lunch ≑ Here's What Happened

# Book **ONE**

## *No Kidding*

They put up R-S-T-L-N-E and only N-E appeared on the board. "It was pretty obvious what that word was: NEW, but it was such an arbitrary word. Anything can be NEW, so I needed some help. I called out my go-to letters H-M-D-O and once again, Vanna stood there motionless,"

"During the time Pat was talking to me, I kept looking at the used-letter-board," said Emilbert de Leon, a certified nursing assistant and mathematics grad from Daly City, California.

He, it must be said, is a member of the *Short-bus-Crew*; a group of (10) diverse individuals – individuals who would never have met, let alone spend every weekday together, talking like old friends while playing (Wheel of Fortune Toss-Up on Twitter) a hangman style game which revealed puzzles one letter at a time, and the winner is whoever tweeted the correct answer first.

Together, the Short-bus-Crew formed a veritable cross-section of economic classes, perspectives, and lived experiences. And that is what made this brief daily encounter, *Special.*

"I've watched Wheel of Fortune since I can remember. My parents would sit me in front of the TV to watch it so I have been prepping for this moment my whole life," Emil said.

The first letters he ever learned were R-S-T-L-N-E, which are the main letters in Wheel of Fortune, but this was the first time he had actually been on a game show.

"I'm not very good at talking at all. I'm such an introvert. I stutter a lot, but when it comes to solving puzzles, I'm in my zone and it gets rid of my stutter," Emil says.

"Uhh... this looks tough to me," the host said to Emilbert. "You are a good player, but I don't know. You have 10 seconds. Keep talking, maybe the right answer will pop out... Good luck!"

Bonus Round (Category: Thing). NE _ * _ _ _ _ * _ _ _ _ _.

Emil faced a nearly impossible task in the bonus round. He only had two letters, N-E, leaving 10 blank tiles. Two words had zero guessed letters. He struck out when he guessed the following consonants and vowel: H-M-D-O.

Although not seen by viewers at home, the game show set includes a used-letter-board that shows which letters still remain in play, a scoreboard, and a countdown clock.

"The B was the first letter there and that stuck with me, eventually forming the word 'BABY' to go with 'NEW'."

"As for 'BUGGY', I thought about what one could find in a baby's room that uses the letters from the used-letter-board, again starting with the 'B' and came up with 'BUGGY'."

"It helped that I am in nursing school, and that month we were studying pediatrics, so I referred to that setting, as well."

"I yelled out 'NEW BABY BUGGY' as my first plausible solution while thinking of other phrases that could possibly fit, but luckily, I didn't need to think of any other phrase."

The category was (thing) so the possibilities were endless, yet Emil managed to pick the correct answer – on his first guess.

"New baby what?" Vanna threw her hands up in disbelief.

It apparently stunned the tech guys as well, because it took four seconds before the solution appeared on the board, and now everyone realized he gave the correct answer.

"Call it the luckiest guess of a lifetime!" TODAY Show's Al Roker said of the solve.

But though Emil was frisked live on-air, TODAY Show's Natalie Morales joked that maybe there were hi-jinks going on.

"I am just saying, it's great publicity for the show, isn't it? We are all talking about it!"

Roker and Matt Lauer poked fun at her conspiracy theory.

Pat Sajak; actor, talk show host, former weatherman and sexagenarian (a person 60 to 69 year old) wrote:

"Tonight's Wheel of Fortune features the most amazing solve in my 30+ years on the show. *No kidding.*"

He then asked if we could keep a secret:

"Please, no spoilers about tonight's incredible solve."

After Emilbert's show was aired, the longtime host added, "What made last night's solve amazing was the generic category. Could have been 'new anything.' But 'baby buggy?!' Wow!"

---

"Beautiful things happen when you distance yourself from negativity." *Mark Anthony Linton*

# Book **TWO**

## *Brown Sugar*

J ust a few scant minutes before puzzle time, I walked into the kitchen looking for caffeine. "Stop!" It's Sabrina's voice. "I JUST MOPPED!" Usually, I screamed back, not this time. Probably because what showed of her legs was silky and smooth, as her daisy-dukes rode up just enough to tantalize, light flowed over her like a blanket that revealed more than it covered.

I leaned down, whispering huskily, "Who's your Daddy?" Her ponytail bobbed threateningly, and her eyes stated what was next. She planted her hands on her hips and said, "Mr. Charlot." That's her father.

I snapped out of it after realizing that the next puzzle was about to start, gave her the-Gas-face, then walked over to pantry on tip-toe so the floor that she just mopped was not made dirty.

"Is there any coffee ina di house?" yuh hear wah mi seh. Translation: Did you hear what I said.

I was born on the island of Jamaica, West Indies in the Parish of Manchester but predominantly raised in Maryland, just outside Washington, DC with a strong Jamaican hand (*literally*).

My mother Somica, a living example of a Godly woman, with the hand-speed to match Floyd Mayweather Jr., whenever Andrew, my older brother by 12 months, ran over her heels with the shopping cart. I have been paranoid ever since and always pay close attention to the way people push their carts.

There's the standard two-hand-stand-up-straight method. This is my method, and it's pretty self-explanatory. Then you've those cart-draggers who walk in front or beside, pulling their cart around. This method is obnoxious because it occupies the entire aisle. The last method is the most fascinating to me. I don't have a name for it yet, but we have all seen it. It's when the driver is laying on the cart, chest and arms draped over the side, and pushing with their stomach.

I speak English without an accent but can certainly speak Jamaican (*Patois*) and may turn the dialect on and off depending on company and conversation.

My uncle Vivian said I speak with a *twang*, a slang term used to refer to a Jamaican who grew up speaking Patois, tries to talk in American accent, but ends up being a silly-sounding poor attempt because it's not natural.

Although I always talk with my older brother Garfield and first cousin Denise in our native tongue, it's still said that I speak Patois with a Yankee accent. "Mark go pan a one-day trip to Merika and cum back with a twang," they all say. Translation: Mark went on an one-day round trip to America and came back with an accent.

I left the island when I was 10-years-old and have been back 4 times (3 funerals, 1 honeymoon) in 32 years. My father, Lascelles, still lives there, but I have no compelling reason to visit after my last trip.

It was the day following my first cousin Ingrid's funeral. I was an emotional wreck and arrived late to the airport. Pulling my carry-on bag, I dashed to the gates, leaping over trash cans like OJ Simpson in the Hertz commercial. It was impressive! One of the skycaps clocked my 100 meter dash at 9.85-seconds, just behind the world's fastest man Usain Bolt, but slightly ahead of Justin Gatlin.

I got to the boarding gate and a long line greeted me. I saw a young woman with a Sangster Airport (MBJ) employee ID card hanging from a lanyard and a (We-Love-Our-Customers) button. I decided to test that theory – "Hi, I think I am going to miss my flight back to Atlanta," I said. After a quick glance at my Air-Tran flight 1057 boarding pass, she replied – "YES, you are!"

Not quite the response I was looking for. I pushed out my bottom lip into a puppy face, letting it tremble slightly, and asked, "Is there anything you can do for me, Sweetheart?"

Her eyes flickered up, cheeks tinged a heavenly shade of pink, as she blinked and suggested using the employee security entrance, even escorting me to the gate, in spite of the dirty looks from other travelers in the cattle line.

My delight quickly turned into a nightmare when officials found a .22-caliber bullet (the shell casing) in the seam of my bag. "A wha- a what?" I stuttered. "I don't even own A gun."

The following 7 hours of my life is a period of time I will never forget and truthfully, never want to endure again.

The young Customs officer invited both me and my trusty carry-on bag into an interrogation room with a *one-sided mirror*. Once inside, he began to inspect the contents of my travel bag.

"Mi cyan arrest yuh right now! Yuh waan fi guh a jail?" he shouted repeatedly. I immediately went into full panic mode.

How could this be happening? What was I going to do?

You can read the rest of the story in my sophomore novel: *The Shell Game* – a memoir that documents the shakedown on the island. I actually finished the book 2 years ago but withheld, since I'm not particularly trilled with the finished product nor am I pleased with the land of my birth.

1pm! It's almost time! No coffee, no tea, no energy drink, and I am getting anxious. This was not an unusual state for me. Between my bustling Real Estate business and picking up my then five-year-old son Markie from kindergarten, I played Wheel of Fortune (often known simply as Wheel) constantly, and Twitter Toss-up was my battleground.

Today was a great day. I was first to tweet correct answer and proudly accepted the Bragging Rights Award for Individual Achievement on a Twitter Toss-Up puzzle. Thanks everybody. Thanks much Short-bus-Crew. Thanks Emilbert & Chad for not playing today. – *"Somebody please get those two on the show!"*

I cannot forget to thank my Grandmother because she is the reason I developed a love for Wheel. I would find myself so affected by the lessons she taught me while sitting on the edge of her bed, one foot shoved into her quilted pink bedroom slippers, watching the most popular syndicated show in television history.

Before she died, I made her a Promise – a Promise that I would get on our favorite show. I was 12-years-old.

My Grandmother raised (6) children and stepped in to raise (26) Grandchildren when parents were absent or unable. Raising a 2nd generation was one of her greatest joys.

She also, it must be said, looked amazing. At 81, her skin had none of the usual bags nor wrinkles. She credited cornmeal porridge for her freakish youthfulness.

She always made it with milk, and I always hated it. Even with a couple tablespoons of *brown sugar* heaped on top, it still managed to taste like warm cardboard.

However, one imagines that part of her glow was derived from her name Emma, which in Arabic means Star, and she took those words as something of a directive.

My daily involvement with Twitter Toss-up underscores something that in retrospect has been evident for a long time, which is that I dreamed of one day being a contestant on Wheel. And not just winning... but winning big!

You would suppose, and be correct that perhaps the best puzzle solvers on the planet could be found on Twitter. I craved the competition with the other players and with myself.

While I'm polite and non-confrontational in everyday life, everything changes when placed in a competitive environment. If I cannot win, I will find a way to feel like a winner.

Yesterday, the Twitter Toss-up puzzle turned out to be VERMONT MAPLE SYRUP. I finished in third place behind Steve & David. - "*Somebody please get those two on the show!*"

I congratulated everyone then started a twitter fight over the category "Food & Drink" which I believe was misleading – leading one to believe the answer contained a food AND a drink.

So, is Maple Syrup a food, a drink, or both?

# Book **THREE**

## *Meet the Crew*

Every weekday, I sat down with ten strangers for lunch, table of individuals chatting away, lost in conversation, never once making eye contact.

1pm! It's almost time! Menus are being passed around as the rest of the merry crew find their seats. We total eleven, including @WOF5K (Wheel of Fortune cast-member).

I set down my Burberry London leather laptop briefcase, pull into the bench, and sit down. I have once again found myself at a table composed entirely of complete strangers who know @SkinnyRealty – but not Mark Anthony Linton.

"Hey, how are you?" asks @GameShow2Go. He's the first to speak. Not entirely sure if it's directed at me, but I returned the gesture. "What's Up!" We talk about my skinny genes and his previous life as a squirrel. These aren't your typical topics when it comes to first meetings – that is what made it, *Special.*

The voice of the former squirrel belongs to Eric Pierce, a broad, hulking five-foot-ten gentleman with a square jaw set just beneath a perpetual frown and a wrestler's neck that looks like a tree trunk. Next to him, my genes looked even skinnier.

Eric appeared on "The Chase" hosted by Brooke Burns. He also appeared on "Who Wants to Be A Millionaire?" hosted by Cedric-the-Entertainer. Coincidentally, the same week as my loan-officer, Tanya Blanchard. She won $64,600. He won $53,500. More than $118,000 and they didn't even buy me lunch.

The L.A. resident and Penn State grad discloses that he is a game show junkie, with a sports problem, and a trivia fetish, and making quite a career of it:

------------------------

Challenge Producer – *Match Game* on ABC

Challenge Producer – *Hip Hop Squares* on VH1

Challenge Producer – *Genius Junior* on NBC

Producer – *Super High Roller Bowl* on CBS

Challenge Producer – *Home Free* on FOX

Producer – *World Serious of Poker* on ESPN

Challenge Producer – *Child Genius* on LIFETIME

Writer – *VMAs Video Music Awards* on MTV

Post Producer – *The Ultimate Fighter* on FX

Production Assistant – *Jeopardy!* on ABC

I can't help but to ask Eric if he got hurt falling through the floor when he appeared on the NBC high-stakes game show, "Who's Still Standing?" hosted by Ben Bailey.

The basic premise is that there is one person (the hero) standing in circle of ten others (the strangers) who the hero needs to defeat in head-to-head trivia battles. There are 11 rounds, with a maximum of 10 duels per round. In each duel, the hero is going to choose his opponent. Everyone stands on a trap-door, and whenever a person loses a duel, *bye-bye.*

The host asks a series of { *Fill in the Blank* } showing the words in the correct answer. The hero is given two passes at the start of game. Passing a question forces the stranger to answer it. The last one standing wins the entire jackpot.

I see my crew-mate on TV wearing a lime green shirt with a puffy charcoal vest, so I tweeted, "Why do I get the feeling that @GameShow2Go is about to rip off his shirt & yell Hulk smash!" Eric replied, "Wardrobe dept. put me in green. Not my fault."

I think I like "Who's Still Standing?" I am finally able to watch a trivia quiz show and know enough answers to feel like I am smarter than the people on the TV screen.

"What is a luxury hotel and a cracker?" _ _ T _.

I've been hungering for a show where Russian Roulette meets Wheel of Fortune's Toss-Up Round. To paraphrase the early, funny, Eddie Murphy from Raw: If you have been starving, a Saltine will taste like a 'RITZ' cracker.

"What one-eyed character was played by John Wayne and Jeff Bridges?" _ _ _ _ E _ * _ _ _ _ _ _ _.

I don't think I like "Who's Still Standing?" Why y'all gave my friend the hardest question ever? He answers incorrectly and a trap-door beneath his feet opened, sending Eric falling through the stage, eliminating him from competition.

The one-eyed Marshal who first appeared in the (1968) novel, *True Grit,* is 'REUBEN COGBURN'.

At other end of the table sit @AgateShadow & @Jadenewt, a warm and gracious married couple from Spokane, Washington with a strange Zamboni obsession.

The boxy four-wheeled contraption is not particularly graceful. It does one job, intermission after intermission, night after night. Yet the Zamboni machine, that overgrown ice-tractor that resurfaces the rink between ice hockey periods and figure skating routines, always elicits pure joy for Jesse & Susie Bush.

"I'm from Houston so I'm a bit of a Texans fan, but I also support the Rangers and the Stars," Jesse reveals.

I share my fondest memories as a Washington Redskins super-fan, watching Doug Williams beat John Elway as a kid and rubbing the logo on my Starter jacket whenever they scored a touchdown. "I rubbed 6 times during Super Bowl XXII," I said.

Susie grins as she listens to myself and her husband cover the usual macho subjects before taking over to guide conversation to greener, more meaningful pastures.

What follows is a remarkable story that began when she was diagnosed with epilepsy in the 3rd grade and placed in special education classes. The classification of being a special education student resulted in bullying inside and outside of the classroom.

---

*"Susie rides the short bus – She might be dangerous"*
She was not impressed with my rhyming abilities.

Teachers labeled Susie as a student lacking the ability to perform well in school, and other students bullied because they viewed her as "different."

All of these stigmas, all these experiences, caused her to develop low self-esteem, low confidence, and a defeated mindset. This would follow her until the age of 19 when she met Jesse online and had an awakening.

Jesse was into sci-fi books, movies, comics, and I dare not say anything about his hobbies nor his Houston Astros, since his favorite team's logo doubles as a symbol of the Tango Blast, a horrifying street gang whose members number well over 17,000 in prisons across the state of Texas.

He fell deep for the young beauty who was enamored with the Spokane Chiefs (WHL) and the New Jersey Devils (NHL). We don't care much for Hockey south of the Mason-Dixon line, so I quickly switched the conversation over to food.

"Hey Skinny! Jesse had an idea! One day when you write a *best-selling autobiographical novel*, come out to Boots-Bakery, an all vegan restaurant in downtown Spokane and do a signing," Susie said. "I will never write a book and I love meat," I declared.

After 13 years of marriage, Susie still beams when she speaks of her husband's encouragement. "Jesse always supported my decision to further my education. Even on those difficult days, he pushed me to keep going. He never let me quit."

Jesse helped Susie complete her high school diploma and led her to an amazing discovery – no longer did she have to fall victim to the stereotypes, victim to the labels imposed by society.

As a result, Susie excelled, obtaining her Associate's, then Bachelor's, and now Master's degree in Psychology with a focus on Child and Adolescent Development from Walden University.

"I'm currently thinking of getting another Master's Degree in Human and Social Services with a focus on Military Families and Culture," she proudly proclaims.

---

*"Susie rides the short bus – She's so smart and fabulous"*
She was still not impressed with my rhyming abilities.

In the ensuing conversation, I learn that the talkative and talented woman to my left is @KimDoyleWille. She's an advocate and activist on behalf of the unemployed, hungry and homeless. The former restaurant owner-manager is also a 14 year veteran volunteer firefighter from El Jebel, Colorado.

Last Monday, Kim was honored to compete in the 46th Pillsbury Bake-off at the ARIA Resort & Casino in Las Vegas where she won the JIF Innovation Award and $5,000 with her Thai Shrimp Pizza, deemed the best recipe using peanut butter. The peanut butter was mixed with orange marmalade. American style pizzas have come a long way from basic pepperoni.

It was with great humility and tears that Kim Doyle Wille admitted to purchasing ingredients for her prize-winning recipe using SNAP (food stamps). My inquisitive side wondered how this came to be, but before I could muster up the right words to ask such a question, she began to unveil more of her story.

In a tragic turn of events, she lost her husband, a popular coach and a member of the U.S. Nordic Ski Team, Raoul Wille to the mountains (altitude sickness) while climbing Mt. Baruntse in the Himalayas of eastern Nepal, at the tender age of 45.

When things couldn't appear to get any worse, Kim later found herself unemployed. During the seven difficult years of unemployment, she came to rely on cheap but unhealthy food and paid the price. Her weight blossomed, her teeth worsened, she was becoming depressed, she wasn't eating fresh produce, and none was available at the pantries. "Obesity and hunger are two sides of the same malnutrition coin," Kim cautioned.

She turned tragedy into triumph and became the founder and executive director of *Growing Food Forward*, a volunteer driven charitable non-profit that reclaims unused space to grow fruits and vegetables, and gives 100% of the produce to hunger relief meal service programs serving children, adults and seniors.

Last year, *Growing Food Forward* was involved with more than 100 gardens and helped supply more than 8,600 pounds of fresh produce to the needy in Colorado.

Through it all, Kim has kept her warm, outgoing, bright, upbeat personality and great sense of humor. She smiled while sharing a memorable moment with me:

"Twenty years ago while I was checking-out at our local El Jebel City Market, *Princess Diana*, dressed in everyday clothes with her princes William and Harry, and a couple of low-profile bodyguards, got in line behind me. We had a brief exchange and Prince Harry chimed in, too"

"At the time, I had shoulder-length hair with exception of a waist-length, thin braid down my back. As I was putting my groceries inside my car, I realized the Royals were near when I heard Prince Harry's voice."

"Mum, did you see that lady's (braid) down her back? Why does she grow part of her hair that way?" the Prince asked.

Princess Diana responded, "I don't know. Harry – why don't you ask her yourself?"

"We ended up having a great conversation, with them telling me how much they loved Colorado, that they had been bowling at El Jebowl (in El Jebel) the night before, were going to go rafting that day, and were enjoying staying at Goldie Hawn and Kurt Russell's house."

"I played soccer with Kurt for a few years, whenever he was in Aspen. The talk continued longer, once Princess Diana learned I played – football."

In the middle sits the vivacious @BeckyLynne1, a retired postmaster and Mary Kay consultant from Saint Clairsville, Ohio. At 65, she's still wildly beautiful, with thick gray hair worn short, and wide uncomplicated eyes.

Rebecca Gray Stead pulled out her cell phone and started sharing photos of her couch buddy, a black Pitbull Terrier named Jemma. She is a rescue dog. It was surprisingly easy to jump into small talk without much anxiety. After all, we're both dog owners.

"I saw a picture of Jemma on a Facebook rescue site and her face just spoke to me. Her eyes were so sad that I could not stop crying, so finally my husband Chris said, let's drive to NYC. I prayed the entire 7-1/2 hour trip. She already had kennel cough and would be killed if no one adopted her quickly."

"We took her home, stopping by Walmart for a crate, bed, and treats. She gets along great with her 8 feline friends and loves being hand fed by our 3-year-old granddaughter."

I learned that Becky lives in a state where she pays taxes, but her dog isn't welcomed. "We enrolled Jemma into obedience classes and were told not to return and again while searching for doggy daycare, we were told – NO PITBULLS!"

But what was Jemma's crime? She was simply born the wrong breed. No one cares if the dog saved a life at some point, served as a search and rescue volunteer dog, or more importantly, if the dog is considered a member of the family.

"These experiences brought back a flood of memories from the 1960's when I argued for integration at debates in high school and was called a N_GG_R * L_V_R," Becky disclosed.

Half a century later and she still stands for the right thing and is now an advocate for responsible, non-discriminatory dog laws and works tirelessly to eliminate Breed Specific Legislation.

With her upbeat personality, one would never surmise that she had overcome a lifetime of tragedy to become the brave and strong woman we know today. Her eyes began to fill up with emotion as she spoke of a sequence of unforgettable moments.

"In 2003 my brother, who was tormented by alcoholism, suddenly died of esophageal varices at the age of 50. His death began a series of traumatic events for mom and I, as my father died 6 months later."

In an effort to lighten the conversation and bring about a smile on Becky's face, I asked the most obvious question of all:

"Can *we ride in your pink Cadillac, crushed velvet seats, riding in the back, oozing down the street.*" My keen knowledge of 80's music brought laughter around the table.

"I haven't received the coveted pink Cadillac, but maybe one day," she said. We began to notice that Becky would abruptly leave lunch. When asked if everything was okay, we learned that again, she showed warrior strength acting as caregiver while her mom courageously fought cancer a second time.

Even though Becky was suffering from previous injuries and Wolff-Parkinson-White Syndrome, a birth defect in which the heart develops an extra electrical pathway which can lead to a rapid heart rate, she did everything to make her mother's life comfortable and enjoyable. Despite all her efforts, Becky's mom died leaving her heartbroken.

"I've always had a tendency towards depression, starting with molestation as a child, aggravated by my troubled marriage, a divorce, then by my physical problems. After my mom's death, I became very non-functional. For three months, I did nothing!"

We all wondered what brought Becky back from such a dark and sorrowful place. Our eyes widened with amazement as we heard the words, "Bees and Wheel."

"Bees?!" We declared in unison. Becky smiled and said "Yes, Bees and Wheel changed my life."

The Wheel-of-Fortune lover in me wasn't surprised by the second half of her response, but I listened intently to learn how a pestering and sometimes dangerous insect could possibly help someone combat depression and loss.

"It started when my mother was receiving home therapy. One day her therapist, a beekeeper, invited us to a beekeeping meeting. I didn't really know much about the process, but after researching the subject, I fell in love with the creatures and we started our own hives."

"Beekeeping became a passion, a newfound joy, and a chance to help others. We gave away a lot of honey and are working on getting the greenhouse operational so we can donate fresh honey and produce to local food pantries."

*Aunt Bee* gives of her time speaking at her niece's high school and enjoys introducing beekeeping to the next generation.

Becky's response to pain inspired us and was a reminder of the famous prose from William Blake's poem:

- *The Marriage of Heaven and Hell*

"The busy bee has no time for sorrow."

I hear a whisper in the wind, a rustling amongst the leaves. "How is everyone doing on this beautiful afternoon?" I quickly knew that it was the clever and caring @InLoveInKC.

Eileen Van Kirk, affectionately known as *Chip* to family and friends, graduated from the University of Kansas and always hollers: "Rock Chalk, Jayhawk!" whenever she would beat us on Words with Friends and Wheel of Fortune Toss-Up.

I've to say hearing the Rock Chalk chant in New Orleans during the Final Four in 2012 was one of the most chilling and awesome things I've ever experienced watching college basketball.

*Chip* works as a computer programmer for American Century Investments, Inc. With such a humble spirit, I smiled as she bragged about her company being named to FORTUNE Magazine's (100 Best Companies to Work for).

"So, what makes y'all so great?" I asked. "Well, on my first day there was a welcome banner, balloons, the whole team came along for my first lunch, and the company treated!" she replied.

The UnderCover-Fat-Kid lurking inside of me smiled as I recited these famous words, first uttered by Abraham Lincoln during the Gettysburg Address: "Show me someone who does not like a free lunch, and I will show you a liar."

---

*Editor's Footnote* - Honest Abe never said that. The author is simply trying to illustrate the timeless appeal of free food.

1-pm EST! It's almost time! I found myself back at lunch, but something was different today. *Chip*, who was always punctual, was not at the table. Instead, we were joined by a gentleman. He makes eye contact with my searching gaze and offers up a wave.

Our lunch guest is *Chip's* husband, Sgt. Bruce Van Kirk. Emilbert recognized the retired 25-year Marine who appeared on 'Wheel Salutes Our Military – Episode 5314'.

His opponent, Naval anti-submarine officer Sarah Feagles from Canton, Ohio won a season-high $42,000 on a single puzzle: Category (Things). B _ RB _ LLS & _ _ _ BB _ LLS. Thanks to those B's and L's ... Sarah solved: BARBELLS & DUMBBELLS.

We all salute Bruce for his service to our country and his appearance on Wheel. "Thank you all, but that is not the reason for my visit. I have come with some sad news."

You never forget that sick feeling. You think about it all the time. I think back to the good times. I think back to the daily Toss-Up battles (usually a losing battle for me), especially on the anniversary – June 25th.

"Dead?!" I screamed in utter astonishment. Her husband starts to { *Fill in the Blank* } on a well-kept secret. *Chip* had been battling pancreatic cancer.

We all wondered how we didn't know and why she did not tell us. My heart tells me that in her loving nature, *Chip* was looking out for the Short-bus-Crew and did not want us to worry.

Reactions at the table varied. Some fell silent. For others, the ocean's currents flowed down their cheeks uncontrollably, ruining anything in their path.

A huge knot formed in the pit of my stomach as I tried to digest the news. I excused myself from table as the feelings of sorrow and dread began to push contents of my stomach upward.

I splashed cold water on my face, thinking it would wake me from this nightmare. The water only removed particles of sweat that had formed on my forehead as it sank in that this was reality. Our precious *Chip* was gone.

We could feel intense emotions as Bruce shared stories with us, "She was the love of my life and stubborn as a mule and very competitive. We could talk about anything," he mentioned.

Bruce and *Chip* auditioned for Wheel of Fortune when Wheelmobile visited Kansas City. "She was a very straightforward type of person but wasn't real outgoing, except with me," he said.

The couple would be notified by mail if they were chosen or hear nothing at all if they were not. After two weeks of anxious waiting, Bruce received the golden letter to be a contestant on Wheel of Fortune; *Chip* did not.

"She was upset she didn't get selected, but happy for me. Ironically, *Chip* was the words person in the family, and I was the numbers person. We did well together. She was a very intelligent woman, and I still love her to this day."

Bruce and Chip's story has taught me that love is such an amazing and powerful thing. Though it overtakes our bodies, death could not conquer the love they shared, and their love personified the words of the legendary Bruce Lee:

*"Love is like a friendship caught on fire. In the beginning a flame, very pretty, often hot and fierce, but still only light and flickering. As love grows older, our hearts mature and our love becomes as coals, deep-burning and unquenchable."*

"Love never fails."

*1 Corinthians 13:8*

# Book **FOUR**

## *Second Place*

The puzzle category was "Movie Title" and one of the contestants managed to sweep through the round and filled in almost all the blanks.

The answer was obvious – 'GONE WITH THE WIND' but the guy kept spinning and building up his winnings. Everyone was relieved when he announced he'd like to solve the puzzle. With confidence, he proclaimed – 'DONE WITH ONE HAND'

Pleasure and excitement for the Short-bus-Crew came from solving puzzles. We each possessed a love for the game, and I suspect it was that passion for puzzles that strengthened our bond and kept us coming back to the table every weekday at 1pm.

Before we could find our seats, I blurted out, "So what did y'all think about last night's show?" The laughs that followed showed that Short-bus-Crew knew exactly what I was referring to.

"I think he was watching the wrong movie," Eric quipped.

Laughter filled the air as we prepared for the main course, Twitter Toss-Up Challenge, which posed an interesting question and ultimately confirmed a sneaking suspicion.

Game-shows are, and always have been all about fun, so when the Short-bus-Crew could not solve puzzles straight away, we would tweet silly answers.

Wheel of Fortune's cast-member, official spokes-wedge @WOF5K thought our screwy solves were entertaining and started re-tweeting. We fought harder to receive a shout-out from $5K, than solving the actual puzzles.

It's every Wheel-watchers dream to have this gentleman, dressed like a "Wheel of Fortune" wedge to come knocking on their door with free money. One lucky viewer will receive a phone call from a local affiliate station asking for puzzle solution from previous episode. If the viewer answers correctly, he or she will receive a visit from $5K, who will hand deliver $5,000!

"People are really happy to see me though. I mean, here's this big shiny thing walking towards you with a smile on his face, giving you money... everyone's happy!" he emphasized.

@CarrieGee, freelance entertainment writer and honorary Short-bus-Crew member based in Ontario, Canada asked $5K, "Now that there are $10K and million-dollar wedges on Wheel, do you worry about your job security?"

"Absolutely not! I will be here forever. I mean, you want to get to the $10K or the million, where you gotta go? You gotta pass me. I've got the sparkles and with the economy the way it is, anyone is happy to land on me. Ten thousand dollars? That may be asking too much. And a million? No, you need $5K!"

Some people have accused him of being in costume, but "This is no costume. This is me. It's all me. I wake up this way! Shiny and fabulous! This isn't my job, this is who I am!" he said.

I leaned over to him and whispered, "I know your real identity! Carter, isn't it? *Travis Carter.*" He gasped and backed away from the table. "What else do you know about me, Skinny?"

Travis is a Producer, Writer, Artist (*T-Rev*), Actor – he's an entertainer at heart. He even had a record deal in high school as part of a boy band in Ohio. He now lives in Los Angeles with his wife and seven kids (Yes, 7) and the Real $5K loves the Lord:

"I'm called to influence the influencers through Christian ministry and my God-given entertainment talents. Stars are role models whether they like it or not. I show them how to embrace the privilege and maximize the benefits through the knowledge of Christ. I love people sincerely and want everyone to succeed. So don't hate...there's room for us all at the top!"

Menus are being passed around as the crew gets ready to play another round of Twitter Toss-Up with the category: "What are you Doing?" G_ _ _ _ _ G * A * G_ _ _ * _ _ _ _ A _ _ _ _ .

I wanted to solve but didn't know what the last two words were, so I jokingly guessed: 'GETTING A GIRL PREGNANT'.

The conversations stop. All eyes on me. I think I have let the cat out the bag. So, I had been keeping a very big secret the past 3.5 months. Sabrina was pregnant with our second son, Dylan Linton, which explained my silly solve.

Another was apparently having the same cerebration, but the Short-bus-Crew had a knowledgeable feel and the looks being exchange at the table told the others, we knew.

"I think there's a cheater in our midst," Jesse speculated. "A cheater! What do you mean?" she replied.

Let's just say, if we could not see the other players tweets, I would have bet on someone finishing last, by a mile. Someone who managed to always finish in *second place.*

"I don't look at Twitter until we've figured the puzzle out," she maintained. I quickly looked over everyone's plate before they could wipe their tweets. I wasn't surprised.

"Hey Short-bus-Crew, take a glance at her one-of-a-kind solution – 'GETTING A GIRL PREGNANT'."

There was a brief moment of silence as the crew digested the information. "There should be a mini-bus for non-cheaters," Emil tweeted. Again, no surprise, he was first to correctly solve puzzle – 'GETTING A GOOD EDUCATION'.

She repeated over and over and over that she didn't cheat and 'getting a girl pregnant' was the very first thought on her mind when the puzzle appeared which made me wonder what exactly the chances were of her 'getting a girl pregnant'?

Unless I missed a great advancement in medical science, I would guess her chances are, you might say, zero.

I reminded her that I just got a girl pregnant and that my silly solve was a way to let the crew know that we were expecting. In addition, the 4th word had 9 spaces – 'pregnant' has 8 letters.

And *second place* for the 7th day in a row? Let alone, the only Short-bus-Crew member to never finish first?

But surely she couldn't expect us to believe it?

She could not, yet there she was, emphatically denying the truth that so directly, so blatantly, stared back at each one of us.

I had to wonder, was winning worth sacrificing character?

We gathered around and stared at results on menu board. Congratulations: @HappySteve @B_B_ @Snowed_In @Emilburp @ChadMosher @SkinnyRealty for solving puzzle.

Coincidentally, the exact order each player later appeared on-air. There are no prizes for *second place*. As Dale Earnhardt once called it, "Second place is just the first loser."

---

"Denial is an ugly thing."

Nicholas Sparks, *Three Weeks With My Brother*

I Sat Home and Watched Four Friends

on Television ⊜ Here's What Happened

# Steven **CHAI** (Contestant 1)

## *$80,350 in Cash and Prizes*

G et ready. First (toss up) coming up – it's (fun & games). SKATEBOARDING. Simple as that – Steven Chai, a programmer from Aurora, Illinois. "Have you ever done any Skateboarding?" Sajak asked. "I have not," he replied. "That concludes this interview. Thank you Steve for being here."

Married? "Yes, to a beautiful wife Niki and we have a wonderful adorable one year old, Max." Speaking of adorable people, you're a big fan of 'Weird Al' Yankovic. "That's correct. My wife and I firmly believe that laughter is the best medicine."

As the first Short-bus-Crew member to actually appear on Wheel of Fortune, Steve was asked the same question over and over: "So, how did you get on the show?" I was more interested in learning exactly how many 'Weird Al' concerts he had seen?

"Don't worry, I'll answer the first question later," he said. Regarding the second question, the answer is invariably: A LOT. But here's a more precise answer: Steve has attended sixty-four (Yes, 64) 'Weird Al' concerts and shows no signs of slowing.

Steve went to his very first concert in 1994, coincidentally, the same year 'Weird Al' was approached by Wheel of Fortune.

He was initially unsure about appearing on 'Music Stars' week until discovering that he'd be playing against James Brown and Little Richard. When it became evident that the 'Godfather of Soul' was having trouble understanding the rules of the game, the show producers teamed him up with Little Richard.

They played as a duo verses Weird Al and country singer, Lee Greenwood, best known for his single "God Bless the USA" which was popular when it was originally released and inevitably became popular again after September 11, 2001. At the end of this incredibly bizarre game, Greenwood beat everybody.

"When I found out Wheelmobile was coming to Chicago, I practically jumped out of my seat. Wheel has always been my favorite show. I was prepared to go to every day of Wheelmobile in hopes of getting picked," Steve stated.

Everyone in attendance was handed a sheet of paper that announced: If name is not selected today, do not worry. Wheel of Fortune will also randomly select names from the remaining applications for the future contestant audition. If you are chosen, you will be contacted via letter or e-mail.

Luckily at the second-to-last drawing of the first day, the host finally drew his name. During introductions, Steve sang a verse of Weird Al's hit – 'White and Nerdy'.

"We played a Speed-Up round which I didn't solve, but that was okay because I had a blast just being there," Steve added.

Afterwards came the toughest part... *waiting*. Two months go by and there's no word. Then finally one day, he gets an email inviting him to a second audition in two weeks.

"I was ecstatic! Soon I was in a large ballroom with seventy other hopeful future contestants," Steve stated.

If you have never been surrounded by Wheel of Fortune fanatics, then you have truly missed out on a magical experience. Those aspiring to reach Sony Studios in Culver City have a sparkle in their eyes and a melody of R-S-T-L-N-E flowing in their hearts.

"First came the written test, which whittled us down to 20. Then 4 at a time, we stood in front of the room pretending we were on the show spinning the wheel, guessing letters," Steve says.

When it was his turn, he made an extra effort spinning the phantom wheel and called out a "T" only realizing a second later that the player before him had just called out the same letter.

"Oh No! I thought it was all over, but luckily the wheel got back to me and I did manage to solve that puzzle plus the one after that," Steve revealed.

"At the end, they congratulated us all and said if we were chosen, we would get a letter or an email in the next two weeks."

"Going home, I couldn't help but to wonder if that one mistake would cost me a spot."

Two weeks later, no such letter appeared. "I was feeling a tad disappointed, then one day I received a surprise call from California asking if I could fly out to Los Angeles in two weeks... I jumped on the table and started singing..."

---

*Happy Days is my favorite theme song*
*I can sure kick your butt in a game of ping pong*
*I will ace any trivia quiz you bring on*
*I am fluent in JavaScript as well as Klingon*

*They see me roll on, my Segway*
*I know in my heart they think I'm*
*white n' nerdy*
*Think I'm just too white n' nerdy*
*Think I'm just too white n' nerdy*
*Can't you see I'm white n' nerdy*

The next 14 days, Steve got into 'Contestant Mode' and watched 'Wheel of Fortune' every night at home.

"I stood up with a clicky-pen at hand for Toss-Up rounds and really pushed my brain to figure out what letter I'd call next at every moment. I read that Ken Jennings, who raked in over $3 million after winning 74 straight games, prepared for his spot on Jeopardy doing something similar – so I figured it couldn't hurt."

"Finally the day came. I got to the studio around 7:30am and the next four hours the other contestants and I went through the legalities of the game and practiced spinning the heavy wheel."

It's the moment of truth. Steve would be playing against:

*Allison Rice* – University of California-Irvine sophomore and an active member-secretary of her sorority (Alpha Phi) from Los Alamitos, California.

*Kathryn Wagner* – Trainer for a software company from San Francisco, California.

I was home in Atlanta, on the blue leather sofa with brass plinth base, watching Steve on TV, eating a spicy beef patty, and drinking cola champagne. It's dark yellow to light brown in color, with a flavor comparable to bubblegum or cream soda, with no connection to cola or champagne.

$1,000 Toss-Up (Fun & Games). SK _ TE _ _ _ _ _ _ _ G. Steve solves: SKATEBOARDING.

$2,000 Toss-Up (Around the House). FLO _ R * _ AMP. Steve's two for two: FLOOR LAMP.

$10,000 Round (Food & Drink). It's a *prize puzzle*, which offers a prize (usually a trip) to the contestant who solves puzzle:

STEAMED * S _ _ IMP * D _ MP _ I _ _ S. In the middle of round, my Short-bus-Crew mate cashes in $7,500 with the M's. Steve solves: STEAMED SHRIMP DUMPLINGS. He dominates winning $10,050 and a trip to Bangkok, Thailand.

Commercial break! Allison $0. Steve $19,750. Kathryn $0. I rushed to the fridge to grab another bottle of cola champagne. Earlier that day, in the Hispanic section of grocery store, right at the end of it, facing the dried chile and tortilla bread, sits GOYA.

Markie sat in the basket while I stocked up on my favorite drink. Pretty sure he only came along because the new Kroger store on Salem Road gives away free "kid's cookies" at the bakery.

Jackpot Round (Event). Allison picks up the jackpot wedge with two S's and a $2,500 gift certificate, but she *Bankrupts* on the next spin and lose $3,450. Kathryn picks up the New Zealand trip with four N's: REGION _ _ * S _ _ ES * CON _ ENTION. Kathryn solves: REGIONAL SALES CONVENTION for $5,200.

Mystery Round (Fun & Games). Allison picks up a gift-tag with two T's and lands on the mystery-wedge but misses with the P. Kathryn then collects $7,500 from the big-money-wedge with three G's but *Bankrupts* on the next spin to lose $7,250.

I screamed "Aitch!" from the top of my lungs scaring our Siberian Husky, Cheyenne, who was napping next to me.

Steve heard my cries and lit up the H's:

A * H _ GH * _ ATT _ NG * A _ ERAGE and solves the puzzle: A HIGH BATTING AVERAGE.

$3,000 Toss-Up: _ _ T _ IN _ _ AM * _ _ G _ A _ _. Category is (On the Map). Steve solves and sweeps the Toss-Ups.

⚡Tough one! (I will let you figure out puzzle for yourself)

Commercial break! I got up to get a third cola champagne. The fridge door was still wide open from last time, pouring cold out onto the floor. Sabrina was standing there, hands on her hips, "Learn to shut the friggin' door!" she shouted.

"I think the dog did it. This isn't a well designed fridge." It's the only explanation I could come up with.

Round 4 (Phrase). THAT'LL * DO * THE * TRI _ _. On his 2nd spin, Steve hits the $5,000 space and lights up the T's for $20,000. He hits $5,000 again and puts up the (D) and solves: THAT'LL DO THE TRICK for $26,400. His new total is $50,350.

Round 5 (People). _ H _ LDH _ _ D * S _ _ _ TH _ _ RTS. Allison finally solves a puzzle: CHILDHOOD SWEETHEARTS.

Final – Kathryn: $5,200. Steve: $50,350. Allison: $6,500.

Bonus Round. In this round, the winning contestant spins a smaller wheel with 24 envelopes to determine the grand prize. He is given R-S-T-L-N-E (Phrase). _ _ T * _ _ R * _ * _ _ N _. Steve calls out: B-G-F-O with puzzle: F _ T * FOR * _ * _ _ NG.

What do we've in the envelope that's FIT FOR A KING like Steve? Another $30,000 giving him a grand total of - $80,350!

"Someone from Wheel of Fortune left a message today. They're interested to hear what I've done with the $80K prize money as part of their (*Changing Lives*) segment."

"Well, I did fulfill my life-long dream to live an entire month on nothing but Slim Jim's and margaritas."

# David **RIGSBY** (Contestant 2)

## *$39,160 in Cash and Prizes*

**A**PRIL 2013 – "Happy Wednesday, Facebook family! My friend David is on Wheel of Fortune. He already won a CAR and has a chance to win a SECOND car! I dig it when friends accomplish their goals. Tune in, if you can."

"I actually forgot that I had applied for Wheel of Fortune. I did so in early 2011, I think, after just completing the *Jeopardy!* online test (and failed it by one question)," David acknowledged.

Last night's Jeopardy! episode was easily an instant classic.

Mr. Trebek: This long-handled gardening tool can also mean an immoral pleasure seeker...

Ken Jennings: What's a Hoe?

Mr. Trebek: No.

Other contestant: What's a Rake?

Mr. Trebek: Yes.

Frankly, I thought Ken's answer was far more amusing and really – just as accurate.

David almost missed the invitation to the Austin tryouts, as it was sitting in his spam folder, with a subject line in all caps, about a year and a half later.

Thankfully, he read it before emptying the folder and decided to take the afternoon off from work as a Design Engineer and headed to the resort where Wheel of Fortune had reserved space. Travaasa Experiential Resort is surrounded by the ancient live oaks and undulating hills of Balcones Canyonlands Preserve.

The resort is brimming with amenities, but David is here for one reason. The audition process would be stressful enough, but he had also come down with a virus which made for a fun afternoon in Texas hill country.

David was in a room with other hopeful future contestants. They filed into their seats and were shown some fun Wheel of Fortune videos to loosen them up.

Then they were given a written test and went on a break. Twenty minutes later the contestant coordinators started calling names of people they wanted to stay.

Before you know it, David's name was called! The room quickly narrowed down to around 20 people and his chances just got a lot more real after making cuts.

They played more games, pretending to spin the wheel, buying vowels and solving puzzles. "I thought it went very well, especially when three other hopefuls and I were called up for a third look. One of them ended up at my same taping session."

"It was about a week later when I got the letter that I was in the contestant pool, six weeks after that when I learned of my taping date, which was less than two weeks away," David added.

"I scrambled to make reservations to get there the week after Thanksgiving."

"Six episodes worth of contestants all met for orientation, taping promos, and getting makeup. I genuinely liked most of the other contestants."

"I wasn't thrilled with the ones who made *nasty comments* about Vanna's appearance after she showed up without makeup in our little briefing."

Those other contestants are lucky David was in that room and not me. Without hesitation, I'd have smashed their faces. For the record, beneath the foundation and highlighting cream, Vanna still looks amazing.

"I felt pretty comfortable playing the mock game before taping started. Our episode was the first to tape of the six that day, so I didn't have long to wait, which was probably good for my nerves," David stated.

I have heard it said that being nervous is not a bad thing. It just means something really important is happening, and this was definitely an important moment in David's life.

"After taping started, I was almost completely unaware of the cameras and just concentrated on playing and listening to Pat and our awesome and very excited contestant manager, Jackie."

The married father of three would be playing against:

*Sandy Wenger* – Chaplain at Univ. Hospital in Cincinnati from Walton, Kentucky. She likes to watercolor paint and write.

*Ben Schwartzman* – UCLA graduate student researching autism from Los Angeles, California. He likes to rap.

I was home in Atlanta, on the blue leather sofa with brass plinth base, watching David on TV, eating a spicy beef patty, and drinking cola champagne. It's dark yellow to light brown in color, with a flavor comparable to bubblegum or cream soda, with no connection to cola or champagne.

$1,000 Toss-Up (People). SE _ _ O _ ED * TR _ V _ _ _ RS. David solves: SEASONED TRAVELERS.

$2,000 Toss-Up: P _ _ _ I _ G * BY * T _ E * R _ LE _. Category (What are you Doing?). My friend is now two for two.

⩶Tough one! (I will let you figure out puzzle for yourself)

$10,000 Round (Proper Name). David picks up the ½ Car. He lands on *wild-card* and calls the (S) then buys the last vowel (A) revealing: SINGER-SONG _ RITER * A _ I _ IA * _ E _ S. David lands on *Jackpot* and calls the (G) then solves the puzzle: SINGER-SONGWRITER ALICIA KEYS.

Commercial break! David: $14,200. Sandy $0. Ben $0. I made a mad dash to the fridge and was disappointed, to say the least. I was hoping to grab another bottle of cola champagne and satisfy my craving for this sugary-sweet, candy-like, refreshing beverage. I need you to picture Birch Beer with Sprees; however, my supply had been diminished. Now what to do?

I dare not go to the store and miss my friend on Wheel.

Mystery Round (Before & After). Ben gets the Caribbean cruise with the (R) then buys the (E) before accidentally repeating the (T). He tries to change to (S), but it was too late.

David follows up with *Lose a Turn*. Sandy calls a bad (G). The Wheel get backs to Ben who tries the (S) again before landing on *Bankrupt*. Back to David who picks up the ½ Car with the (L): MY * HOUSE * IS * YOUR * HOUSE * SALA _ .

David solves: MY HOUSE IS YOUR HOUSE SALAD.

He only won $950 ... but has both Car-tags and wins a Smart Car!

Prize Puzzle (Rhyme Time). Ben *Bankrupts* out the gate. David then calls a bad T. Sandy calls M then repeats the bad T. *Bankrupt* hits Ben again. David calls R then buys an O revealing: I'M * _ OO _ ING * O _ ER * A * _ O _ R - _ EA _ * _ _ O _ ER.

⚓Tough one! (I will let you figure out puzzle for yourself)

He only won $800, but *Prize Puzzle,* and a trip to Ireland ($5,880)

$3,000 Toss-Up (Show Biz). THE * BIG * SCR _ EN.

David solves: THE BIG SCREEN.

Round 4 (Food & Drink). I was back on the blue leather sofa, upset because there was no cola champagne in the house, but happy because David was doing great on Wheel of Fortune.

I hear *final-spin* sound while my absurdly large flat-screen TV flashed, every evening, at the exact same time. I took that as a sign that Grandma is safe in Heaven watching Wheel with me.

That ship's bell sound-effect means we don't have much time, so Pat will give the wheel a final spin, then ask for a letter, vowels are worth nothing and consonants are worth...

Hearing that sound brought back a flood of memories from Grandma laughing like water in a pleasant streamlet and pinching my right arm when Pat's final-spins landed on *Bankrupt.*

(Patois) Me: "Him lan pon it." – Grandma: "A weh yuh a seh?"

(English) Me: "He landed on bankrupt." – Grandma: "Really?"

David calls N. Sandy calls D. Ben calls R. David calls S. Sandy calls G. Ben calls T. David calls A. Sandy calls W. Ben calls E revealing: STR _ NG * _ _ _ _ EE * AND * SWEET * TEA. Ben solves the puzzle: STRONG COFFEE AND SWEET TEA.

Final Scores – David: $39,160. Sandy: $0. Ben: $6,200. As the show headed into commercial break, I was excited to see how my crew-mate would fare in the bonus round. Thinking about his winnings so far, I'm sure that I wasn't the only Wheel-watcher wondering how, and if, David would fit into a Smart car.

While fitting his 6 foot frame in the compact car may have proved to be a challenge for David, fitting his entire world inside the Smart car seemed to be a far easier and more rewarding task.

His only regret as he walked across stage to bonus-round was that his lovely wife (Karin) was unable to make the trip from Texas to California because they had a two-month-old at the time.

Bonus Round (Thing). S _ _ RT * _ _ _ _. David calls out H-C-D-O. The *wild-card* gave him an extra consonant which he used to call the (P) now revealing: SHORT * _ _ _ _.

David did not solve the puzzle: SHORT QUIZ for the Mazda Miata and missed out on winning a second car.

"I had what had to be the worst bonus puzzle of all time, but I didn't let that ruin my day. I couldn't wait to call Karin and tell her that we just won a trip to Ireland and a brand new car!"

I turned off the TV proud of all David accomplished. As I sat on the blue leather sofa, it dawned on me that he was the second Short-bus-Crew member to spin the big wheel. I smiled, looked up, and said, "I know it was you God."

I smiled even bigger as I wondered who would be next.

---

"Don't wait until you've reached your goal to be proud of yourself. Be proud of <u>every</u> <u>step</u> <u>you</u> <u>take</u> towards reaching that goal." *Mark Anthony Linton*

# Emil **DeLEON** (Contestant 3)

## *$63,099 in Cash and Prizes*

**M**ARCH 2014 – "Happy Wednesday, FB family! My friend Emil is on Wheel. He already won a trip to CABO and heading to bonus-round with $18K! I dig it when friends accomplish their goals. Tune in, if you can."

June 2013 (Facebook messenger). "Hey Boogie, guess what?" I said. "Sup man?" Emilbert replied. "I uploaded a video and got email back the same day from Wheel of Fortune inviting me to an *invitation-only* audition," I said.

"That pose at the end of your video got me. Haha. I've no doubt in my mind that you will get on the show," Emilbert said.

"Thanks Boogie, I think I WILL, and I think YOU need to try-out since you're the best solver I've ever seen," I conceded.

"Thanks Skinny, but with my schedule for the next year or so... AIN'T NOBODY GOT TIME FOR THAT... But if I did have a break in school, I'd totally do it! Give me a year+ or so..."

August 2013 (two months later). "I heard Wheel-mobile was coming to Jackson Rancheria Casino in the Sierra foothills. My mom, dad, grandma and great-grandma accompanied me, mostly because the audition was being held at a casino and you know grandmas and casinos," Emilbert says.

"I made sure to arrive early, about noon, to find myself and my mom 10th in line. As time went by, the line grew longer."

"So came 2pm, we were escorted inside the ballroom, filled with about a thousand chairs, all of which were soon packed with enthusiastic Wheel-watchers. Everybody got situated and we took pictures next to the Pat and Vanna cardboard cut-outs. As soon as everyone took their seats, Marty (the faux Pat) and Morgan (the faux Vanna) came to the stage."

"Marty called names up five by five in the first audition, and my name was nowhere to be seen, so my mom and I returned to the second audition," Emilbert murmured.

"Marty called names five by five again. After nine round, our names were nowhere to be found. My mom and I were not planning to stick around for the third audition."

"First name -not me. Second name -not me. Third name -not me. Fourth name -Emil. What?! Did I just win the lottery?! I was chosen second-to-last. I blurted my celebratory 'WooHoo' then gave my phone to my mom to record it."

Category is (Before & After). _ _ _ _ _ _ * _ _ _ _ * _ _ _ _. He was 4th in line, and when it was his turn, Emil called out his favorite initial letter (R) revealing: _ _ R _ T _ * _ _ _ _ * S _ _ _.

Surprisingly, Emilbert did not know the answer and the other players bought four vowels: _ ARATE * _ _ O _ * SUE _.

⚡Tough one! (I will let you figure out puzzle for yourself)

"They told us we would get a call-back within three months if we made it to the next round. And here begins the long and tedious wait for the next call-back," Emil says.

After his first audition, Emil spent every day checking his email and spam email to make sure that he did not miss out on this opportunity of a lifetime: "I knew they said within 3 months, but like that spoiled kid from Charlie and the Chocolate Factory, I WANTED IT NOW!"

October 2013 (Facebook messenger). "Hey Boogie, guess what?" I said. "Sup man?" Emilbert replied. "Eric got on Who Wants to Be a Millionaire?" I said.

"Now that's awesome news! GO Eric GO! Any word on your second Wheel audition?" he asked.

"NADA word. They quickly weeded out the room after the written test and I was one of the final 20. It was really fast. You only get to call a few letters so they'll not know that you're a great puzzle solver. They only want to see that you understand the basics, so you MUST call vowels. They love that. LOL." I joked.

"I'm never stopping. I've a friend that got on-air after her 7th audition, so I am just getting started," I added.

"I see myself writing a best-selling book in a couple years about the Short-bus-Crew, so I need you to get on the show and break-the-internet. I truly believe it WILL happen..." I predicted.

October 2013 (two weeks later). Emil was overjoyed at the sight of an email: Wheel of Fortune Audition in Jackson, CA. Emil, his mom, his grandma, and his great-grandma saddled-up for another trip back to Jackson Rancheria Casino.

The crew of four-generations decided to stay overnight so as to avoid waking up early and having to rush to arrive on time.

"The time came and we were escorted to a much smaller ballroom with 100 or so seats, only about 70-80 of which were occupied by final-round contestants," Emil estimated.

The first puzzle showed up and my crew-mate knew the answer with ZERO LETTERS ON THE BOARD but could not solve since he knew casting executives wanted people who struck a good balance between calling consonants and buying vowels. Movie Quote: _ _ _ * _ _ _ * _ _ _ _ _ * _ _ * _ _ _ _ * _ _ _.

Emil spun his heart out, then called out the R-T-H-B and bought an (E) before the judge purposely landed on *lose a turn* leaving the puzzle: _ _ _ * THE * _ _ R _ E * BE * _ _ TH * _ _ _.

⚡Tough one! (I will let you figure out puzzle for yourself)

Everyone had a chance at smiling, clapping and solving puzzles, which led to the next portion – the dreaded written test.

If there is a time during the audition for you to show-off, this would be it. Emilbert was the first to finish with enough time on the clock to double, triple, and quadruple check his answers.

The casting executives exited the building to grade tests, leaving a big room full of nervous people, 20+ minutes to mingle.

"I talked to a few people about how they did on the test and the results were all over the place. Some said they got 5/16, some said 7/16, others 4/16 – I felt good."

"After the break, they told us that they were going to make cuts and eliminate people based on test results and puzzle play in the beginning. They cut probably 40-50 people, leaving about 20-30 to fight it out. My name was finally called towards the end, and of course, the suspense was killing me!"

"They then told us that we would play a mock round, but we must be quick, ready, and it would be intense," Emil added.

They had 2 puzzles in his group. Emil was able to solve 1. Then similar to the first audition, they were told to give a 15-20 second blurb about themselves: "Emil, Daly City, Nursing student, love to travel, karaoke and couponing," he repeated.

That was the end of his audition and they were told that letters would be mailed in 2 weeks to those selected for the show.

2 weeks later, Emil received THE letter: "Congratulations! You have been selected as a contestant on Wheel of Fortune."

"December 16, 2013 – I received an email which sparked the beginning of the actuality that this was happening. I read the heading: Wheel of Fortune taping on Friday, January 17, 2014."

"The day started for me around 5:00am since we had to be in the studio at 6:15am. This is where I met a handful of fellow Wheel-watchers who were set to be contestants. I have to say that these were some of the nicest, most down-to-earth people I have ever met. The fact that we shared a love for Wheel of Fortune just made our bond even tighter, but it slowly dawned on me that 2 of these new friends would become my competitors," Emil realized.

Then contestants were debriefed and prepped on game rules, terms, and conditions. They had refreshments and mingled a bit, before *signing away their lives* – not to die, but to live a dream.

"We were assigned in groups of three, which pretty much showed match-ups in each episode. Then we picked numbers to decide which show each group would appear. Numbers 1-5 were 'European Vacation' and number 6 was 'America's Game' week."

"I was appointed the ball-guy at random for my show and voila, I chose number 6... last episode, longer wait. I didn't know whether to feel depressed or relieved," Emil said.

"We then chose positions, and I chose #1 (red position) right next to Pat. We were also told ahead of time about the trip offered for our episode, and it was a trip to China."

The contestants were given a chance to practice puzzles, try out the signaling devices, and of course spin the BIG wheel.

"It looks much smaller than on TV!" Emilbert revealed.

They were escorted to their own section of the audience and since Emil selected number 6, his group would watch every episode. After the third episode, they were given a pizza break.

"It was the very best pizza I have ever had, mostly because I was getting restless and still had to sit through 2 more episodes."

It's the moment of truth. Emil would be playing against:

*Charlene Gibson* – Adjunct professor in public speaking from Las Vegas, Nevada. She has lived in Japan and Germany.

*Kendra Bacon* – Special Ed. teacher from Lawrence, Kansas. She has been married for one year and participates in roller derby.

I was home in Atlanta, on the blue leather sofa with brass plinth base, watching Emil on TV, eating a spicy beef patty, and drinking cola champagne. It's dark yellow to light brown in color, with a flavor comparable to bubblegum or cream soda, with no connection to cola or champagne.

$1,000 Toss-Up (On the Map). P _ _ _ _ IX * _ R _ _ _ _ _. Charlene solves: PHOENIX ARIZONA.

"I am not going to lie. I was pretty much paralyzed at the fact that I was up there. Vanna was across the stage. Pat was right next to me. I just could not focus on the puzzle," Emil admitted.

"The interview was the most nerve-racking part for me. I hate talking. I am such an introvert. Pat went through everything on my card, but it was still the shortest and most awkward ever, mostly because I did not expect him to talk about karaoke. I had a lot of other things on my card: Giants fan, traveling, couponing. Karaoke was something I tossed on the back burner as a hobby. Thank God the interview is over," Emil sighed.

$2,000 Toss-Up: _ _ _ Y _ _ _ * _ _ _ R _ * _ _ _ _ S. Category is (What are you Doing?). Emil solves his first puzzle.

≜Tough one! (I will let you figure out puzzle for yourself)

Puzzle board was showing Y-R-S, leaving 14 blank tiles. This was far more challenging than the puzzle with 10 blank tiles Emil solved in bonus-round that made him a YouTube sensation.

15 MILLION views – but am I the only person to notice ?

"I probably could have used more letters, just to be sure, but I rang in and solved the puzzle – with ONLY 3 LETTERS!"

"I can tell that some of the media didn't watch the entire episode if their sole focus was on the final bonus round puzzle. This was a really sound solve as well," Emil pointed out.

Round One (TV Title). Emil calls T-L-W and buys O-A, revealing: W _ O * WA _ T _ * TO * _ _ * A * _ _ LL _ O _ A _ _ _.

Emil solves: WHO WANTS TO BE A MILLIONAIRE. "I knew the solution so not sure why I bought the A?" Emil said.

Mystery Round (Thing). Kendra picks up EIGHT (T's) revealing: THE * PITTE _ * PATTE _ * _ _ * LITTLE * _ EET. Kendra then solves: THE PITTER PATTER OF LITTLE FEET.

"I was a bit worried, but she landed on small-value wedges which saved my lead. She won $4,850 and ½ Car-tag," Emil said.

Prize Puzzle (Place). _ OO _ TO _ * IN _ INIT _ * _ OO _. Emil solves: ROOFTOP INFINITY POOL. He only won $400 but it's a *prize puzzle* so he is going to Cabo San Lucas, Mexico.

$3,000 Toss-Up: _ R _ N _ _ _ _ H _ R * _ LOC _. (Around the House). Emil solves: GRANDFATHER CLOCK.

Round Four (Phrase). SOUNDS * A * _ IT * IFF _. Emil bought O-U-I then calls an F and solves: SOUNDS A BIT IFFY.

Round Five (Event). ANN _ AL * _ _ _ PAN _ * P _ _ N _ _. "I'm glad Charlene solved so we all won something," Emil stated.

≢Tough one! (I will let you figure out puzzle for yourself)

Final – Emil: $18,099. Kendra: $4,850. Charlene: $4,400. I dashed to the fridge to grab another bottle of cola champagne. I popped the cap off and was greeted by a cloyingly sweet smell then scurried back to the blue leather sofa just in time to hear Pat ask: "Who do you have in the audience?"

Emil's grandfather, parents and brother are in attendance. He spun bonus wheel, passed the envelope to Pat, and stood on the marker which started the 5 minutes that would change his life.

Bonus Round Puzzle (Thing). NE _ * _ _ _ _ * _ _ _ _ _.

"I yelled my first plausible solution: NEW BABY BUGGY and thought of other 'NEW BABY' items using the letter-board, but luckily I didn't have to think any further since it appeared on the board. I pretty much lost it. I couldn't believe what I just saw. I couldn't believe what I just did. I never expected this to happen."

"Pat showed the $45,000 and I was pretty much just over-joyed. My family then rushed onto the stage to congratulate me."

"Back home in Daly City, we had a get-together (30-40) friends and family, all gathered around the television to see how I did on the show," Emil said.

"I could hardly function properly the entire day, especially since Sajak tweeted a *spoiler* about the show early that morning."

"The party was a huge success. Everyone cheered, yelled, a few picked their jaws up off the floor at my unbelievable solve."

"And to top it all off, someone baked me a Wheel cake!"

The following day, Emil became a viral internet sensation. 13,718,333 views – Wheel of Fortune's YouTube channel. 1,757,361 views – The Ellen Show's YouTube channel. 15+ million total views! 100's of media outlets across the country ran stories on Emil's amazing puzzle solve. He also made appearances on the following:

---

The Ellen DeGeneres Show

Thirty Mile Zone *aka* TMZ

Late Show *with* David Letterman

Inside Edition – CBS Television

The Today Show on NBC

Good Morning America on ABC

Jimmy Kimmel Live on ABC

"Hey Skinny, I love how I looked back at my Facebook messages and I seem to always go back to the one where I direct messaged... so you want me to audition for Wheel of Fortune?"

"AIN'T NOBODY GOT TIME FOR THAT... I'm in school... and then I turn into such a liar who ends up on the show. I guess I did have time for that."

---

"Relationships are the most important thing in life and friends are a part of that." Nicholas Sparks, *Three Weeks With My Brother*

# Chad **MOSHER** (Contestant 4)

## *$19,450 in Cash and Prizes*

**F**EBRUARY 2015 – "Happy Tuesday, Facebook family! My friend Chad is on Wheel of Fortune. He already won a trip to PARIS and heading to bonus-round with $19K! I dig it when friends accomplish their goals. Tune in, if you can."

"This is my FOURTH major game show appearance and I'm forever grateful that producers of these programs keep putting an average-looking blonde kid from Flint, Michigan on their TV shows," Chad uttered.

"When he was 3-years-old, he'd walk around the house with a pencil in his hand pretending to be a game show host," said his mother Cathy.

April 2002 (the 12-year old) spotted a contestants-call 4 hours away in Ohio. After consulting with his mom, he submitted an application. A few weeks later, they received a call inviting him to take the qualifying test.

"In a room of about eighty-five, I was one of nine to have passed the thirty question test. After they cleared room of those who didn't pass, I participated in a quick mock game of *Jeopardy!* They took our pictures and told us that we would be contacted sometime in six months if we were to be chosen," Chad revealed.

In late September, the local station that carried *Jeopardy!* called his house and asked if they could come out to his school the next day to do an "interview" about the *Jeopardy!* process.

"That day the news team, along with my principal and mother, informed me that I had been chosen as a contestant to participate in 'kids' week. Thank goodness there was a wall behind me when they told me, otherwise, I would have fainted," Mosher acknowledged.

*Jeopardy!* took great care of them; five-night stay at the Beverly Hilton in Los Angeles, along with $600 for food and incidentals. All the contestants gathered in the restaurant area of the hotel that morning, loaded up into the Sony bus, and took off.

"They were taping five episodes that day, and interestingly enough, my episode was the last of the week, against the two girls whom I had made friends with," Chad revealed.

"Truthfully, I could say that I was not nervous because I had been preparing for this my whole twelve-year life," he added.

"I had done fairly well throughout the show, though my lead was harmed badly when the girl beside me, Madeleine, ran one category on the *Old Testament*," Chad said.

Perhaps the life-lesson here is to read your bible, children. You never know when you might need to cash in.

Unfortunately for Chad, the scores were very close at the end of *Double-Jeopardy*. He had to definitely know what he was doing in the Final. The Category: 'Non-fiction Books'. The Clue: "The Road to Middle Earth was a book written about this author."

"The very first thing that entered my mind? OH CRAP!!! I truthfully had no idea. Amber, the girl on my left, had no guess. She wagered $5,000 thus dropping to $5,800. Madeleine, the girl on my right, had a big smile on her face," he said.

She guessed "Who is Tolkien?" Chad had never read the 'Lord of the Rings' books and didn't know answer.

Madeleine wagered $15,000 thus was now up to $30,300. You could see the disappointment on Chad's face as the camera showed his answer. He risked enough to finish in second place, but nevertheless, victory went to someone else.

"I left with $2,000 and a brand new computer, though the $31,200 I would have won (if I was right) would have been nice! And even through the end of high school, almost six years later, I was known at school as – *That Jeopardy! Kid*."

July 2008 (now 18-years old). "Never in a million years did I even think about trying out for the *Million Dollar Password*. I was planning on trying out for Who Wants to Be a Millionaire when they came to Detroit in mid-August. But by some form of serendipity, I was able to take part in the most curious and best four weeks of my life," he said.

Chad designed his own PowerPoint version of the game, where one could control and host the game in his own home with his own words. He posted it on the Game Show Forum so other fans could download and play. He received the following email:

"Hi Chad, my name is Jill. I'm a contestant producer for *Million Dollar Password*. My senior producers asked to contact you. They saw your PowerPoint version of MDP and were very impressed. We would like to personally invite you to the audition. We are holding an audition in Chicago on Saturday (July 19th). If you have any questions, feel free to email or you can call me directly at (###) ### – ####. Please do not publish that number."

"We were ushered into a ballroom. I filled out the 5-page application and the release form. Guidelines for proper game-play are reviewed (clues that are allowable - those that are forbidden). We were given a (5) word test. They came back and read names of everyone who passed. (Yay, I got called!)" Chad says.

"We then paired up with another applicant and played the game in front of a contestant coordinator in a separate room. You have to get your partner (or have your partner get you) to say five of the passwords in thirty-seconds or less. My partner (Russell) and I, set a day record, getting five words in seventeen seconds."

They would get a call back that same night to come back if coordinators were impressed with game-play and personality. At 6pm that evening, Chad got a call.

"Back to the hotel the next day, with significantly less people in the ballroom. We played in front of the camera and a contestant coordinator. Also sitting there was the main producer (big difference from yesterday!) We played a few more games and then I played the waiting game..." Chad stated.

"I certainly hoped to get a call that week, and if it turned out I didn't make it, well, hey... *Who Wants to Be a Millionaire* was holding auditions in Detroit in two weeks."

"To my enjoyment, Jeremy from *Million Dollar Password* called at 4:16pm on Wednesday, July 30th. I flew to Los Angeles that Saturday. In studio early Monday, where there are 14 other players, with 8 slots for taping?" Chad estimated.

The first taping featured his game show idol, *Betty White*. He was really hoping for an opportunity to play along with her. After five-hours of waiting, Chad was called to play in the final game. As they were checking his mic, the great *Regis Philbin* walks up to him and shakes his hand.

"It took a few seconds for me to realize, 'Holy crap! I just shook hands with Regis!' For the record, he's got the softest hands of anyone I have shook hands with."

Julie Chen (Big Brother) and Phil Keoghan (Amazing Race) are the celebrities he would play with. Chad made the game look easy in the early rounds. Julie could be seen on-air saying, "wow" while watching Chad fire off answers.

When playing for $1 million, Chad cleared the first two rounds in a dramatic face off with Phil. The star collapsed to the floor after finishing the round that would guarantee Chad $25,000.

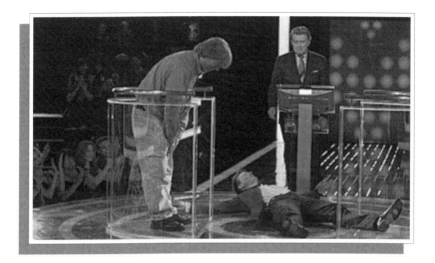

Chad won the 350,000 amount easily, then put it all on the line to play for $100,000 after getting encouragement from the audience.

Phil struggled with the final word (sheet) when trying for the $100,000 prize. Chad's clues included (blanket) and (thin) but Phil could not come up with the answer. Chad still walked away with $25,000.

"Phil was still apologetic about what happened, but I assured him it was okay. As I walked into the green-room, a staff member (*Anthony*) said I was the best player he had ever seen. Truly the ultimate compliment on this trip."

Summer of 2011 (now  21 and legal). "My friend Rich Weingartner and I decided to take a trip to Chicago to audition to be contestants on *Who Wants to Be a Millionaire,*" Chad stated.

As they ventured on this 270 mile (buddy road trip) from Flint to Chicago, the duo began tweeting their statuses, often using @MillionaireTV, the official Millionaire twitter, in messages.

Imagine my surprise when I spotted a tweet saying that my game-show GURU friend was heading out to another audition:

"@SkinnyRealty: Good luck bro!! Short-bus-Crew will be cheering you on!! RT: @ChadMosher: Leaving for Chicago in a few hours to try out for @MillionaireTV."

They arrived and made it into the line around ten minutes to eight. After fifteen minutes of waiting, an associate producer came outside and yelled; "Is there a Chad Mosher in the line???"

"Somehow, I didn't hear my name being called, but luckily Rich did. He sprang into action, as good friends do, and shoved me to edge of line while getting the attention of the producer."

She asked both Chad and Rich to step out of the line and then shared news that was music to their ears. They were being moved to the front of the line because of their road-trip tweets.

Chad and Rich tweeted themselves ahead of the crowd. Donald Trump tweeted himself into the White House. Do not underestimate the power of Twitter and other social media forums, at least until the next innovation comes along.

"Rich and I thought that maybe we would be brought just close enough to ensure we got into the next session. We, along with a few others, and a couple who won a WGN contest, were literally the first ones in line for the next session," Chad revealed.

"The producers told others in line that maybe they should start tweeting, and they would later bring in more people who made unique tweets. I thought that was a fantastic way to reward people with an interest in the show and the audition," Chad says.

Chad and Rich passed the first test and were waiting in line for the next step. Promotions crew did an on-camera interview with the duo. They discussed road trip, tweets, past experiences and how they felt being at the audition.

"I am not sure if it was because of my boyish good looks, or another benefit of our awesome tweets, but I was pulled out to do another off camera interview. Ironically, the interviewer was the associate producer that advanced my place in line earlier."

"We were told promos were not related to the audition, but I couldn't help but think it helped make a great impression with the staff. Weeks later, I discovered my instincts were correct as I flew out to be a contestant on the show," Chad acknowledged.

Chad & Rich went on an epic quest to satisfy more than a craving for White Castle's tiny burgers. Chad received the golden postcard to be a contestant on Millionaire. Rich did not. At least his car was not stolen by *Neil Patrick Harris*.

"My game started a little rougher than I would have liked, as I didn't know that a (sham) was an ornamental pillow covering - it was a hunch, not a certainty, so I *polled audience*," Chad said.

Naturally, with a 95 percent poll result, he was now sure. He pocketed a little money on that question and the next was another stumper that he had to use a *jump the question* lifeline.

"Two lifelines on the first two questions was not how I anticipated the game starting, but it was what it was," Chad cried.

He made it through four more questions ranging from what makes the State Maine unique (one syllable) to the Latin translation of car company Volvo (I roll).

"A couple questions later was the double money question - I knew (Fahrenheit 451) was about book burning so I locked it in. Even if my bank was divided in half, a consequence of walking before tenth question was answered correctly, that was still an amazing amount of money to leave with."

At the time, as an aspiring author in the process of writing *The Shell Game* - when I first heard the question... I cringed!

Meredith Vieira: In the dystopian society of "Fahrenheit 451," which of these businesses would be burned to the ground?

A: Raymour & Flanigan

B: Abercrombie & Fitch

C: Smith & Wollensky

D: Barnes & Noble

"I was thinking 'Holy Crap, I won $50,000' but I obviously couldn't say that on TV but it was incredible," Chad pointed out.

A few more questions passed by where Chad could show off his knowledge of schoolyard games and the alphabetical order of states, pocketing more cash.

With $85,100 in his bank, the next question appeared:

"Everybody's talking about Bagism, Shagism, Dragism, Madism, Ragism, Tagism is the opening lyric to what 1969 song?"

"I had an immediate hunch that this was *John Lennon's* 'Give Peace a Chance'. I had recently developed an admiration for *The Beatles* and some of their solo works, so I had acquired some of their music, including the aforementioned song."

How sure was he that this was the song? Sure enough to risk a large amount of money and move on in the game?

"Apparently so, because after 2 minutes of deliberation, I locked it in as my final answer and was right!" Chad mentioned.

"This led to the last question in round one. Immediately it hit me, I had no idea what the answer was. Fortunately, it didn't cause me to overthink anything or lock myself into an uncertainty – I knew it was time to walk away with half of my bank."

"I won $43,550! Meredith Vieira is the kindest person I met in show business. Her support is one of the main reasons I look upon this experience fondly," Chad acknowledged.

February 2015 (now 24-years old). After acing the final audition in Detroit, Chad was easily selected to appear on Wheel. The substitute teacher and quiz-bowl coach would play against:

*Casey Yudovin* – The co-owner of a perfume company in San Francisco, California. She's originally from Thousand Oaks.

*Erin Vilardi* – Runs a non-profit for women who want to run for government, has a boyfriend who lives in West Africa, and everyone in her family has the nickname Eddie. She lives in NYC.

I was home in Atlanta, on the blue leather sofa with brass plinth base, watching Chad on TV, eating a spicy beef patty, and drinking cola champagne. It's dark yellow to light brown in color, with a flavor comparable to bubblegum or cream soda, with no connection to cola or champagne.

$1,000 Toss-Up (Fun & Games). _ _ NNIS * _ _ TC _. Chad solves it: TENNIS MATCH.

$2,000 Toss-Up: _ _ _ _ Y _ * _ H _ * S _ _ _ _ _ * _ _ N.
Category (Character). Chad solves with 4 letters and 14 blank tiles.

≢Tough one! (I will let you figure out puzzle for yourself)

"Pat made a joke about me liking women shaped like *Olive Oyl* that unfortunately got cut from the show," Chad stated.

Round One: STREN _ TH * AN _ * _ _ E _ _ _ _ _ _ T _.
Category is (Things). Chad: STRENGTH AND FLEXIBILITY.

Commercial break! Erin $0.00 Chad $7,550 Casey $0.00

"In our second conversation, I noted that even though we have different political leanings, I still actively follow Pat's *Twitter*. He noted that it is not all about the politics. I concurred. Vanna was just surprised Pat had A Twitter follower," Chad says.

Mystery Round (Before & After). Erin calls (S), buys (E) and (A), calls (R), buys (I) then finishes with the (D) thus revealing: _ASE_A_ _ * DIA _ _ _ DS * ARE * A * _IR_'S * _EST * _RIE_ D. Erin: BASEBALL DIAMONDS ARE A GIRL'S BEST FRIEND.

Prize-Express Round (Place). Erin calls (S), buys (E), calls (N), buys (I), calls (R), buys (O) and (A) to clear the vowels. She calls (F) then *Bankrupts*. Chad calls out the (C) and (T) revealing: FRANCE ' S * COS _ O _ O _ ITAN * CA _ ITA _ * CIT _. Chad solves: FRANCE'S COSMOPOLITAN CAPITAL CITY.

"I kept spinning even though I knew the solution to the *Prize-Puzzle* because there were still multiple letters to be had and I hate when people solve with no money and just win a trip."

"Looking back, I don't think the strategy to keep spinning in *round-four* was that great. I wanted to hang onto control in case the *final-spin* bell rang, so that way I would finish the round with the solve. But maybe I should have just solved with a couple thousand and went to *round-five* where more money could have been had and I would be next-in-line for control? We all know what they say about hindsight though!"

$3,000 Toss-Up: _ E _ N _ _ * B _ T _ _ R * _ A _ _. Category is (Food & Drink). Casey solves her very first puzzle.

≑Tough one! (I will let you figure out puzzle for yourself)

Round Four: (Phrase). Casey calls (T), buys (E), calls (H), then calls a bad (A). Erin *Bankrupts.* Chad lights up (R) and (N) before *Bankrupts.* Then Casey *Bankrupts.* Erin calls (C) and (D) then calls (F) revealing: _ NE * F _ R * THE * REC_ RD * _ _ _ _ _. She solves: ONE FOR THE RECORD BOOKS for $2,900 more.

Final Score – Erin: $9,350. Chad: $19,450. Casey: $3,000.

"Looks like you came here to have a good time," Pat said.

"I did!" Chad acknowledged.

"You are doing just that and doing very well. $19,450 in cash and prizes. Who's out in the audience with you?" Pat asked.

"I've my friends Julie, Ivory, and Kelsey," Chad replied. They all look like they could easily be cover models for the latest Vogue or Harper's Bazaar magazines.

"Well, you certainly hang in interesting circles," Pat joked.

Chad spun the bonus-wheel, passed the envelope to Pat, then made the short walk across stage and stood on the marker.

Bonus Round Puzzle (Thing). _ _ _ _ _ _ R _ * _ _ _ E _ _. Chad calls out C-H-D-A revealing: _ AC _ _ ARD * _ A _ E _ _.

BACKYARD MAKEUP is Chad's only guess. He doesn't solve – BACKYARD GAZEBO for $32,000. End total: $19,450.

"A very good night, by yourself, at least," Pat jokingly said.

"It may come off as greedy, but I really wish I had won more. Almost $12,000 and a TRIP to PARIS (a value of $6,050 + $1,500 spending cash) is obviously nothing to sneeze at and I'm very appreciative for the opportunity and the reward, but here's why I get a little frustrated thinking about it..."

"My friend (A.J.) gets the show a half hour before I do, and for a couple years he has sent me the show's nightly bonus-round and I give him my own picks for the letters," Chad stated.

"Nearly all my life, playing Wheel of Fortune simulations of all varieties, I've picked C-H-D-A and in the bonus-round. Not necessarily because of coincidence of it spelling my name, but because they're common letters that, for me, frequently help fill in hints for word structures that lead to me solving the puzzle."

"In the last year or so, I'd average that I am .850 to .900 when it comes to bonus-round batting average. Because of this, I'm disappointed I couldn't solve my bonus-puzzle," Chad added.

A recent *Washington Post* article that analyzes data states G-H-P-O is the way to go. But if Chad had picked either of those, he would've gotten: B _ _ _ _ _ R _ * G _ _ EBO (B-G-H-O) or _ _ _ _ _ _ R _ * G _ _ E _ O (G-H-P-O) instead of what he got with his own selection: _ AC _ _ ARD * _ A _ E _ _ (C-H-D-A).

"The recommended choices may have given me *Gazebo*, but would've left me stuck on *Backyard*, a tricky compound word, making it inverse of my situation (getting Backyard not Gazebo)."

"The point of all this is to help myself resign the fact that unless I picked something like B-Y-G-O, I probably wasn't going to be able to solve it. I was assigned a bonus puzzle that was in the 10-15% range that I just wasn't gonna get," Chad concluded.

"Okay... enough whining and post-analysis. I was on the friggin' Wheel of Fortune! And I'm a Champion! And I'm going to Paris! Again, thank you so much for watching me," Chad said.

"If you were cheering and yelling at your TV for me, that means a ton to me. Thank you all. If you were sitting in the dark, yelling obscenities and throwing candy wrappers at the TV every time I solved a puzzle, at least you helped the viewership."

———————

"When you chase a dream, you learn about yourself. You learn your capabilities and limitations, and the value of hard work and persistence." Nicholas Sparks, *Three Weeks With My Brother*

# I Took a Chance and Auditioned for a Game-show ⚏ Here's What Happened

# Book **NINE**

## *Wheel-mobile*

**A**nyone can be unhappy when things aren't going well, but it truly takes a *Duppy* – a malevolent spirit or ghost referred in Jamaican folktales to be unhappy when things are going great.

At thirty-something, I had a successful real estate career, 2 kids, 1 wife, had sex on a fairly regular basis, lived in a massive 4-bedroom house sitting on 2-acres, with a 4-car garage for my Range Rover HSE Sport SUV, Audi Cabriolet A4 Convertible, collection of Polaris ATVs and other predictable extravagances.

This should be ample reason to feel good, but underneath it all, I was still haunted by the promise made to my grandmother.

I had never forgiven myself for being one cocky son of a bitch during the Wheel of Fortune audition in Charleston. By the time I finally began to understand how badly I blew my golden opportunity to be on the show, it was too late.

Every time I think I've gotten over it, I find myself waking in the middle of the night, punching myself so hard you'd think it was only yesterday – not five years ago.

I spotted a tweet that Wheel-mobile, a yellow Winnebago that travels across America in search of contestants for the show, was passing through South Carolina. I bribed Sabrina with a pair of sky-high thigh-high Vince Camuto boots to take the 600 mile, 10-hour round-trip from Atlanta, Georgia.

Over 4,000 people showed up in front of Dillard's at the Citadel Mall as the Wheel-mobile team passed out forms asking: name, date of birth, home phone, work phone, address, email, occupation, what is your SPIN I.D., what are your hobbies, what particularly interesting, fun or unique qualities do you possess?

Sabrina filled-out her form with my name in an attempt to stuff-the-ballot. Everyone who filled-out a form was placed into a spinning bin, like lottery ping-pong balls, and then a lucky few won a spot on stage.

Each would-be contestant is subject to an easy interview with the traveling Pat Sajak (Marty Lublin) who always asked, "What do you like to do in your free time?"

An older lady during my audition answered, "My husband and I have been super into kayaking lately."

The audience only heard the first two words 'My husband' to which Marty yelled, "Keep it clean folks!"

The interviews can take a long time because if you say you sing, rap, or cheer-lead, you are subject to performing that skill.

Whenever said skill were mentioned, Marty always says, "Did you say SING?" and the would-be contestant would be off to the races. I heard *John Lennon's* (Imagine) at least four times.

An hour-long Wheel-mobile event allows for 10 games, (10 games) X (5 names) = 50 folks would get called up for the day.

My odds of getting called on stage were 50/4000 (1.25%). Only ONE percent. I drove 600 miles with 2 wild-loud-screaming toddlers to a shopping mall packed to the brim for ONE percent.

My odds skyrocketed to a whopping 100/4000 (2.5%) thanks to my ballot-stuffing 'partner in crime'.

Come 2pm and everyone was ready. Marty in Pat's role and Morgan Matthews (the traveling Vanna White for Wheel of Fortune Wheel-mobile) came to the stage. They showed the same enthusiasm one would have if they mixed Red Bull, 5-Hour Energy, and a quad-shot from Starbucks.

Their excitement was contagious and the entire audience matched their enthusiasm. Names are called out five at a time. Once on stage, you tell the audience a little about yourself and fall back in line to play. On stage is an upright carnival style wheel. Marty then spins the wheel to show what fun prizes you will win; blinky pin, fanny pack, key-chain, t-shirt, cooler-bag, backpack, and other show related goodies – no cash prizes.

You play a puzzle similar to the Speed-Up puzzle round on Wheel of Fortune where you get one letter, a chance to solve, and it's the next person's turn to play.

Marty started calling names and mine was nowhere to be seen. 5 – 10 – 15 – 20 – 25 – 30 – 35 – 40 – 45. I was getting ready to just call it a day, when I heard – Mark Linton. "Who is that?"

I am pretty sure it was the form Sabrina (stuffed) because I go by *Mark Anthony* and write my middle name on everything. Sh... I mean, I was chosen in the last group of five. I thanked God, kissed the wife, hugged the kids, high-five'd everyone with their hands out, before rushing towards the stage.

There was a tent next to the stage where representatives from the local TV station broadcasting Wheel had us sign waivers.

"Hi, I am *Mark Anthony Linton*, I am a real estate agent from Atlanta Georgia, I have two kids, one wife, and I love to eat, but will NEVER eat another meal till I get on Wheel of Fortune."

I'm 6'5, 165 pounds. Marty just laughed and said you sir should not miss any meals before turning and warning audience: "Do not try what he said at home or you will die!"

A Wheel of Fortune letter-board appeared in front of us, except it was filled with flippable (8 x 10) dry erase white-boards, as was the used-letter list. If a letter is guessed correctly, Morgan aka Vanna flips over white-board and uses a dry erase marker to {*Fill in the Blank*}. Nothing hi-tech, just a Sharpie.

The Category was (Same Name). I was on stage with a fun group of people. We laughed our way through the puzzle revealing: _ ELL _ * AND * SNOO _ E * _ _ TTON. The young lady to my right then calls out (B) and we all knew at that moment she would solve the puzzle: BELLY AND SNOOZE BUTTON.

Congrats Tara Berry, but solving puzzles was not the goal on this day; it was to make an impression on the casting crew. This was the personality portion, and I was memorable.

Tom Spain (*The Post and Courier*) emailed this message: "Mark, I know you're not local so I dropped a copy of our paper in the mail. You made front-page! Enjoy your 15 minutes."

On the drive home through the beautiful South Carolina countryside, we went through several small, yet very quaint towns and passed a couple juicy, tempting veggie-fruit stands, but our wild-loud-screaming toddlers would not give permission to stop.

I turned on some 90's Rap to drown out the screeching noise coming from the backseat and said a silent prayer of thanks. Ok, I didn't really pray, but refraining from losing your cool and slapping two screaming kids counts as a prayer, right?

A colorful and beautiful double-rainbow formed as we entered Georgia and crossed Lake Oconee. I took that as a sign that good news would surely follow this trip as double-rainbows are promises of peace and a sign that the storm is departing.

Sure enough, I received an email the following day saying I passed the first audition and should come back for a second.

Both kids were sick with the "crud" (fevers, coughing, et al) all weekend so we decided that it was best to keep them at home.

I sat behind the wheel of my Range Rover, idling outside the garage, trying to decide which route to take for my second, 600 mile, ten-hour round-trip from Atlanta to Charleston...alone.

---

*Editor's Footnote* – Wheel of Fortune strongly discourages you from incurring any expenses whatsoever; loss of wages, air-fare, hotel, baby-sitter, car rental, etc. in order to try-out for the show.

The TomTom GPS mounted on my dashboard was not working so I went back inside the house to print driving directions from Mapquest. "So you scared or something," Sabrina spouted. "NO Silly! I need to print directions," I said with a half laugh. "You have a nice day," I said softly, affectionately even.

I wanted to tell her that I was scared, but I was already back in my truck turning onto Salem Road towards the highway. It's eight-thirty A.M, Monday morning, still rush hour, but I'll be heading east on I-20, towards Augusta, against traffic.

I reached into the heap of CDs scattered on the passenger seat in search of the perfect road-trip music. It's important to have at least one song in your vehicle anyone can sing along to. *Biz Markie's* (Just A Friend) is that song, that actually gets better the worse you are at singing it:

---

*You, you got what I need*
*but you say he's just a friend*
*and you say he's just a friend, oh baby*
*you, you got what I need*
*but you say he's just a friend*
*but you say he's just a friend, oh baby*
*you, you got what I need*
*but you say he's just a friend*
*but you say he's just a friend*

Five hours later I arrived at the Charleston Place Hotel (Riviera Theatre). There were 70 people and we filled out a more extensive form than the first audition, which included questions such as, "Have you ever committed a felony, DUI, etc?"

Glad to say that I answered NO to both questions.

Then we watched a video on the overhead projection with past winners and bloopers. We all laughed from start to end.

One of the casting-directors started calling us one-by-one to speak our names clearly so they could make a seating-chart and explained that we would be playing a fast game of Wheel.

Then came the moment of truth. We would be shown a puzzle. A judge would call one of our names, and much like the real show, we would spin, buy a vowel, or solve the puzzle.

Once they have seen and heard what they needed to see, they would *Bankrupt* or *Lose a Turn*, since they had control of the fake Wheel, and justly would get to see everyone play.

I was the third to be called and I jumped out of my seat with a big smile because I knew the answer and for some reason, still unknown to me today – I wanted everyone to know I knew:

Category (*Proper Name*). _ _ T _ R * _ _ _ NN _ * _ E _ _.

"Would you like to spin or solve puzzle?" the judge said.

"Do you want an answer or the truth?" I replied.

"Would you like to spin or solve puzzle?" she repeated.

"Easy ... it's ACTOR JOHNNY DEPP" I replied.

I didn't stop smiling, clapping, cheering the other players. We were then given 16 puzzles to solve in 5 minutes. I talked with everyone in my section and scores varied; some said 4/16, some 8/16, one guy got 0/16, pretty sure I got at least 14/16, and just prayed to God that my five seconds of cockiness were not enough to knock me out of the game.

After the casting directors graded our tests, they returned and announced that they were going to call out names and those whose names were called get to stay, everyone else had to leave.

They called 15 names. *I was not one of them.* The hotel clerk validated my parking ticket and I rode down the elevator to the garage. I sat behind the wheel, paralyzed by disappointment. Idling, I did not want to go back home.

I know it's probably in bad character to blame others for your problems, but I am fairly certain that it's all the judges fault. I drove 20 hours, 1200 miles, made it onto the front-page of the largest newspaper in South Carolina, solved an ambiguous puzzle, and scored highest on the written test.

Stalling again, I messaged Chad the scenario and asked what the chances were to still get a letter.

"Sorry bud, but it's nearly impossible. Scratch that. It IS impossible to get a letter to appear on Wheel of Fortune if you do not make the cut during audition... but hey, there's tons more game shows in the country!" Chad said.

"Thanks much. Don't like your answer but appreciate that you take time to answer every question submitted to form-spring. Maybe if I tweet the question, the answer would be different? And there's no other game show," I added.

Twenty enduring hours. One thousand two hundred long miles. Five short seconds of stupidity. It's over. But I knew I had to go home, and put on a happy face, and tell a happy story. Because when you have a wife, and two kids, that is what you do.

---

"Tough toenails, tiger. What you want and what you get are usually two entirely different things."
Nicholas Sparks, *Three Weeks With My Brother*

# Book **TEN**

## *Invitation-only*

I received an email: "Congratulations! You've been selected to attend a WHEEL OF FORTUNE contestant audition by (*invitation-only*) at Omni-Atlanta-Hotel in CNN Center. This would be my THIRD time auditioning for the game-show.

First audition (Charleston 2011). Beat incredible odds at Wheel-mobile, but I was annoyingly self-centered, self-absorbed, and did not deserve the letter.

Second audition (Atlanta 2013). Brilliant, almost perfect audition, but I was somewhat depressed, at the end of my tether, and did not care for the letter.

Sabrina woke up one clear Friday morning, packed up the black Volvo S60, with my two children but not the dog, and left 700 miles north to Pennsylvania. Atlanta has 80,000 more single women (age 18-64) than single men – largest such gaps in the country. I think I will be fine.

But I can't imagine life without Markie and Dylan. I look back on times before them with wistful boredom. I thank God for thinking enough of me to place two blessed kids into my life. Now they were gone. I lie in the dark, alone in this big house on a big chunk of land, the reasons people move to metro Atlanta.

I joined Spirit Airline's famed $9 Fare Club (actually cost $59.95 for the first year). I decided flying to Pennsylvania every two weeks to see my two sons would cure depression.

There's no substitute for raising your children under the same roof, and I never did score a flight for $9. A 60-day trial membership once cost $9, hence the outdated name.

I was willing to pay a price, both physically and financially, to see my sons. 36,000 feet above ground, I received an email message to a second (*invitation-only*) audition in Atlanta. I never doubted that this third opportunity of a lifetime would happen.

August 2015, four years after Charleston, two years after Atlanta (*part one*), and ONE day before my 42nd birthday.

Finally happy, I quit my job and moved from my 2-acre mini-mansion in the country to a 2-bed townhouse in Smyrna and my metamorphosis to entrepreneur left me satisfied.

Finally content, I accepted it. I'd never again hold status as full-time parent to Markie and Dylan. I wondered if stories I read them are the same stories their mom reads them. Now, I stop wondering. You get good at blocking out bad thoughts.

I was now determined not to carelessly discard this third chance faith afforded me. My crew-mate Eric worked on many game-shows, so I asked him for advice and he kindly responded:

"Start off being friendly with everyone there. Eyes are on you from minute one. Smile, shake hands and hug – even fellow potential contestants."

"You want me to hug folks I'm vying for a spot against?"

"Just play the game, spin first, then get a consonant, then immediately buy a vowel, or two. Do not solve the puzzle too fast. It's not a Twitter game. Just play the game, do it with some gusto, and react to everything."

Getting picked to appear on Wheel is hardly a simple task. It requires a good amount of preparation and plenty of luck. What is luck? Whenever I don't know the answer to something, I look to God. What does the Bible say about luck?

*Ecclesiastes 9:11-12* says – "I have seen something else under the sun: The race is not to the swift or the battle to the strong, nor does food come to the wise or wealth to the brilliant or favor to the learned; but time and chance happen to them all."

Pastor Keith G. Nation (Stockbridge, GA) taught me that much of what Ecclesiastes shares is from perspective of a person who looks at life on Earth without God, or life "under the sun."

From such a perspective, leaving God out of the picture, there seems to be good luck and bad luck.

I remember watching Super-Bowl-42 at home in Atlanta, on the blue leather sofa with brass plinth base, eating a spicy beef patty, and drinking cola champagne. It's dark yellow to light brown in color, with a flavor comparable to bubblegum or cream soda, with no connection to cola or champagne.

American Idol season-six-winner, Jordin Sparks sang the National anthem. I met her earlier that year, at the Wolf Creek Amphitheater in Fulton County, and gave her my phone number. She said she'd give me a call but never did.

The Patriots had the first undefeated regular season in 35 years while the Giants limped into the playoffs with a 10-6 record.

The Giant's QB Eli Manning eluded a swarm of Patriots in the backfield (a minor miracle since Eli cannot scramble) then launched a pass deep downfield. David Tyree caught the ball and pinned it against his helmet. He caught the ball with his helmet! A few plays later, Manning found Plaxico Burress for the game winning touchdown and the biggest Super Bowl upset of all-time.

Was it a matter of luck? From an earthly perspective, that helmet catch may seem to happen at random, but throughout the Scripture it's clear that God is in control of all His creation and is able to take random acts of natural law to accomplish His good.

*Romans 8:28* states – "And we know that those who love God all things work together for good, for those who are called according to his purpose."

On the morning of the audition, I was a ball of nervous energy, and my stomach was in knots. I sat on the edge of my bed gazing into the eyes of a determined man, reflecting on my previous auditions, and pondering all the things that could happen in today's audition.

I reminded myself that it was only four years ago that cockiness and arrogance proved to be my downfall, but I was certain today would be different. After all, I was different.

They say that second chances aren't given to make things right, but are given to prove that we could be better after falling.

This would be my SECOND, *second chance* and I was determined that today would be the day that my dream became a reality. Today would finally be the day that I fulfilled the promise that I made Grandma 30 years ago.

Since watching Wheel is one of my daily rituals, it wasn't surprising that my real estate partner, *Alexis London* developed a liking for the show and decided to accompany me to the final audition in Downtown Atlanta.

Her cousin, award winning singer-producer, *Gerad Logan* was visiting from London and said the three scariest words you will ever hear – "Can I drive?"

That afternoon I asked my higher power, Jesus Christ to "Take the Wheel" and keep us on the RIGHT side of the road. I tossed him the keys to the Audi and hit the road to my audition.

I got to the hotel forty-five minutes before auditions were scheduled to begin. I stopped by *Morsels,* the hotel coffee shop, and grabbed a bag of M & M's which helped to settle my nerves.

After turning in our paperwork and head-shots, the casting executives began the lightning round. Category (Before & After). One of the judges asked if anyone could explain that category. Emilbert shared a story with me about his audition and was asked the same question. I quickly raised my hand and was called on.

"Before & After consists of two phrases-names combined by a word that ends the first and starts the second," I answered.

I won an autographed photo of Vanna White. Ironically, the same prize I won at my first Atlanta audition, so I gave it to a wonderfully tattooed lady (Vanessa Fennell) seated next to me.

Everyone in the room gave a great impression during the first phase. Next was the dreaded written test. We were given 16 {*Fill in the Blank*} to solve in 5 minutes.

Quick math - 16 puzzles divide by 5 minutes (300 seconds) $300/16 = 18.75$ seconds per puzzle. Emilbert received a perfect score (a very rare feat). That was my goal.

Similar to Charleston's audition, I solved a puzzle during the first phase but celebrated in a more controlled manner with a variation of fist pumps (Tiger Woods style), high and low fives. I befriended everyone in my row and was glad all made the cut, including the girl with the dragon tattoo.

"Happy Thursday, Facebook family! I auditioned today for Wheel of Fortune. About 80 people were invited to try out in Atlanta. Some dressed to kill, a couple were dressed to thrill, many wore jeans. I went with navy trousers and a khaki blazer. Over 60 were cut after the written test. Luckily, I made the cut and got to stay and introduce myself to the casting executives."

"Hi, Mark, Real Estate Agent, 2 kids, 1 wife, I love to sky-dive but won't do it again until I cross Wheel off the bucket-list."

"I got to spin the imaginary wheel, called the (N), bought vowels, solved the puzzle. That was it. I was done for the day. Letters will be mailed out in two-weeks to those who made it."

As I was leaving the ballroom, a casting executive shouted "How old will you be tomorrow, Mark Anthony?"

"It'll be the 16th anniversary of my 26th birthday. I decided back in 1999 I was no longer going to age," I joked.

I make my way to the car enjoying what I just experienced.

―――――――

"Never forget that anticipation is an important part of life. Work's important, family's important, but without excitement, you have nothing. You're cheating yourself if you refuse to enjoy what's coming." Nicholas Sparks, *Three Weeks With My Brother*

Try Your Hand at Solving the Hardest

Puzzles in Wheel of Fortune History

# Book **ELEVEN**

## *Toughest Solves*

Subsequent pages include puzzles from the 15 bonus-rounds out of over 2,000 in case-study, in which the fewest number of letters were revealed, and the contestants still managed to guess correctly.

--------------------------------

Armed with the same letters, see if you can solve these puzzles in the short, 10-second window. Answers on reverse pages. Good luck!

# FILL IN THE BLANK

33% of the letters are visible

Given letters: R S T L N E

Guessed letters: M P G A

You Have 10 Seconds to Solve

15th Hardest Wheel of Fortune Solve of All-time!

CATEGORY: PERSON

30% of the letters are visible

Given letters: R S T L N E

Guessed letters: C H D A

You Have 10 Seconds to Solve

MARK ANTHONY LINTON

12th (tie) Hardest Wheel of Fortune Solve of All-time!

30% of the letters are visible

---

Given letters: R S T L N E

Guessed letters: F H C A

You Have 10 Seconds to Solve

12th (tie) Hardest Wheel of Fortune Solve of All-time!

30% of the letters are visible

------------------------------

Given letters: R S T L N E

Guessed letters: D G M A

You Have 10 Seconds to Solve

12th (tie) Hardest Wheel of Fortune Solve of All-time!

29% of the letters are visible

---

Given letters: R S T L N E

Guessed letters: M D P A

You Have 10 Seconds to Solve

9th (tie) Hardest Wheel of Fortune Solve of All-time!

29% of the letters are visible

Given letters: R S T L N E

Guessed letters: G D M I

You Have 10 Seconds to Solve

9th (tie) Hardest Wheel of Fortune Solve of All-time!

29% of the letters are visible

Given letters: R S T L N E

Guessed letters: H C P A

You Have 10 Seconds to Solve

9th (tie) Hardest Wheel of Fortune Solve of All-time!

CATEGORY: THING

25% of the letters are visible

Given letters: R S T L N E

Guessed letters: C M D A

You Have 10 Seconds to Solve

4th (tie) Hardest Wheel of Fortune Solve of All-time!

# FILL IN THE BLANK

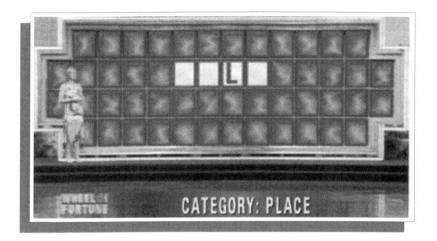

CATEGORY: PLACE

25% of the letters are visible

Given letters: R S T L N E

Guessed letters: D P M O

10 sec

You Have 10 Seconds to Solve

4th (tie) Hardest Wheel of Fortune Solve of All-time!

25% of the letters are visible

Given letters: R S T L N E

Guessed letters: C M F A

You Have 10 Seconds to Solve

4th (tie) Hardest Wheel of Fortune Solve of All-time!

25% of the letters are visible

Given letters: R S T L N E

Guessed letters: B M K O

You Have 10 Seconds to Solve

4th (tie) Hardest Wheel of Fortune Solve of All-time!

# FILL IN THE BLANK

CATEGORY: PHRASE

25% of the letters are visible

Given letters: R S T L N E

Guessed letters: C H W A

You Have 10 Seconds to Solve

4th (tie) Hardest Wheel of Fortune Solve of All-time!

22% of the letters are visible

---

Given letters: R S T L N E

Guessed letters: F P D I

You Have 10 Seconds to Solve

3rd Hardest Wheel of Fortune Solve of All-time!

20% of the letters are visible

---

Given letters: R S T L N E

Guessed letters: D M P A

You Have 10 Seconds to Solve

2nd Hardest Wheel of Fortune Solve of All-time!

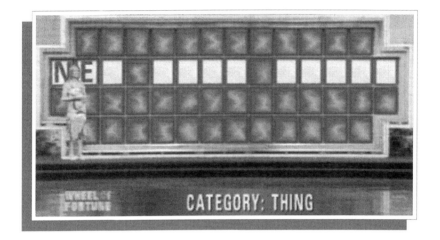

CATEGORY: THING

17% of the letters are visible

Given letters: R S T L N E

Guessed letters: H M D O

You Have 10 Seconds to Solve

MARK ANTHONY LINTON

The Hardest Wheel of Fortune Solve of All-time!

# Book **TWELVE**

## *Over-analyzing*

B EN BLATT, Slate Magazine's Contributor and the Co-author of, "I Don't Care if We Never Get Back" conducted a case study that proved Short-bus-Crew member Emilbert de Leon's (NEW BABY BUGGY) was indeed the most amazing puzzle solve in Wheel of Fortune history, from a statistical perspective.

A word about Blatt's process: His analysis was limited in its scope by the solutions recorded on various Wheel of Fortune bonus-puzzle archive websites.

These websites have recorded almost 13,000 puzzles from the game show's opening-rounds and over 2,000 bonus-rounds going back to 1988. These sites are maintained by viewers, and there is no official record keeping for the show.

His analysis is dependent on accuracy of these super-fans. That said – they all seem extremely committed.

As regular Wheel-watchers well know, the bonus-round in which (NEW BABY BUGGY) happened, operates different than the regular-rounds of play. Since a rule change in 1988, contestants have been given the letters R-S-T-L-N-E automatically. Contestants are allowed to guess three additional consonants and one additional vowel.

This should be great news for contestants, as R-S-T-L-N-E represent approximately 45% of letters in a standard English text.

However, of the more than 22,000 letters in bonus-round puzzles used in Blatt's study, R-S-T-L-N-E only account for 29.6% of all letters – a statistically significant discrepancy.

| | Baseline | Wheel of Fortune |
|---|---|---|
| R | 6.0% | 5.1% |
| S | 6.3% | 3.9% |
| T | 9.1% | 4.9% |
| L | 6.8% | 4.6% |
| N | 4.0% | 3.6% |
| E | 12.7% | 7.5% |
| | 44.9% | 29.6% |

For obvious reasons, Wheel of Fortune's producers seem to be choosing words and phrases that are light on R-S-T-L-N-E, at least in the bonus-round.

During the regular-rounds, R-S-T-L-N-E show up as often as you would expect them to. In his sample, the total frequency of R-S-T-L-N-E was 44.7%, nearly identical to 44.9% you would expected in the standard English language writ large.

After R-S-T-L-N-E are revealed in the bonus-round, player gets to request four additional letters. The (N) and the (E) that showed in (NEW BABY BUGGY) obviously came from the free letters that all bonus-round contestants are given.

For his additional consonants, Emilbert selected H-M-D and (O) for his additional vowel, netting him no additional letters in the puzzle. Was he unwise for picking H-M-D-O ?

If Emilbert were to pick letters purely by their frequency in the English language, he should have guessed H-D-C and A, similar to what fellow Short-bus-Crew member, *Chad Mosher* selected for his bonus-round puzzle, instead of H-M-D-O. But the difference in frequency between M-C and O-A are not huge – at least in real life.

Recall, however, that bonus-round answers do not have the same letter frequency that you find in the English language.

The three consonants and one vowel that show up most frequently in the bonus-round puzzles are H-G-B-O.

Picking H-G-B-O in all past bonus-rounds would have netted players 3% more letters revealed than picking H-D-C-A.

This is very useful information for contestants. (O) is the *fourth* most popular letter in the language, with a frequency of about 7.5%, but it has a frequency of over 9.6% in the universe of Wheel of Fortune bonus-rounds.

Even if you split the bonus-round sample chronologically into five equal samples of 400 puzzles, in order to test for random blips over time, (O) is still the most popular letter in all samples.

The fact that (O) appears far more frequently than letters that usually best it, like E-T-A, suggests that its high frequency is likely not random.

Historically, if all bonus-round contestants guessed the combination of H-G-B-O at every opportunity, the four letters would have revealed 22.5% of all bonus-round letters.

In reality however, contestants rarely guess H-G-B-O, and sometimes guessing strange combinations of unlikely letters like P-K-W-I or J-Z-W-I.

Based on letter frequency in the bonus-round, statistics would suggest that their guesses should have revealed only 18.5% of all letters.

However, contestants' guesses has actually revealed 21.9% of all letters, not far off from the 22.5% that the H-G-B-O advice would yield.

It appears contestants are making educated guesses based on what R-S-T-L-N-E has already indicated about a given puzzle.

That said, every letter counts. Emil came up empty with his guess of H-M-D-O. If he had guessed the most frequent letters, H-G-B-O, he would have been looking at: NE_ * B_B_ * B_GG_.

Ultimately, Emil did not need the help. But for most contestants, those letters might have been the difference between winning $45,000 or going home empty-handed.

Maximizing number of letters revealed greatly increases your chances of winning. For example, contestants who revealed 75% of puzzle letters when the final 10-second countdown starts (players have 10 seconds to solve the bonus round puzzle, with unlimited guesses) go on to guess the correct answer 83% of the time. Even a below average or mediocre Wheel of Fortune player can likely solve a puzzle like: BUS * R_UTE.

When Short-bus-Crew member Emil was presented with NE_ * _ _ _ _ * _ _ _ _ _ , roughly 17% of letters in the phrase were visible. Only about 30 people had every been in similar position to Emil – that is, with less than 20% of letters revealed, and NOT one of them had managed to solve the puzzle.

Blatt's analysis is based on the available data and doesn't date back to Wheel of Fortune's debut in 1975. But based on his sample, it's safe to say that (NEW BABY BUGGY) is probably the most amazing solve ever, from a statistical perspective.

When you consider that 'New Baby Buggy' is a phrase few people have ever heard, let alone would offer up as a guess were they standing in Emil's shoes, the guess is even more remarkable.

---

"Stop getting distracted by things that have nothing to do with your goals." *Mark Anthony Linton*

God's Grace is an Everlasting Source
of Comfort ⸕ Here's How I Know

# Mark **LINTON** (Contestant 5)

## *$50,515 in God we Trust*

**W**e finished auditions and were told, "If selected, you'll receive a letter in the mail in two weeks." From there, I started to wait; I started to *pray*. That 4 letter word 'wait' proved to be such a grueling task because it was during this period of waiting that my mind began to wonder. It drifted deep down into parts of me unknown to others as doubt forced me to ask myself difficult questions:

Did I smile enough? Did I call out letters with a strong, clear voice? Should I have bought more vowels? Was I relatable? Did I show enough personality or was it way too much? Did they mistake my confidence for cockiness? Did I do something wrong to ruin the chances of me reaching my dream?

Pain jilted throughout my head as these thoughts swirled around and around and around as though they were in a blender, forming an unappetizing mixture of uncertainty.

I decided to lay down for a while in an attempt to ease the pain and take my mind off things. I unfastened my Ralph Lauren button-down shirt and laid it neatly on the chair next to the bed. I smiled briefly as the ceiling mirror above the bed reflected the results of the hard work that had been put in the gym.

As I began to empty the pockets of my gabardine trousers, something caught my eyes. It was a small flier that I had removed from the windshield of my car earlier in the day. On it were eight powerful words: "BE STILL, and know that I am God."

Far too often we engage in internal struggles while God is calling us to stop worrying and be still. Our ability to heed this call shows our willingness to trust God, in spite of what we may feel. When we're still and surrender to God, he assuages our fears and provides us with sweet peace and enrapturing joy.

Now 3 months after my 3rd audition, I did something so unexpected, something that would be a complete shock to those who knew me. I sat down on the blue leather sofa with brass plinth base, eating a spicy beef patty, drinking cola champagne, as I've done many times, but this time not for laughs or glimpses of my favorite show. Instead, I rested on this source of comfort and relaxation, pulled out my tablet, and started to write.

Trusting God is extremely hard. If you find someone that suggests otherwise, *RUN* and *RUN* quickly because they are not being honest. It requires us to follow the unseen into the unknown and believe His word against all that we see or the fears we feel.

Where would I begin? What would I say? Would anyone listen? For me, writing was definitely the unknown and parts of me wanted to question why I was about to embark on such a path.

Other than exchanging some witty banter with my peers, my last writing experience was painful as I recounted the horrific events that made me less than proud of the country I call home.

It's not everyday that one has to contemplate the idea that the land of their birth concocted an elaborate, yet illegal plan to procure money from unsuspecting visitors.

With such controversy and great possibility of not being well received by friends and family, I withheld releasing memoir. Would this be a similar experience? Where would I begin? What would I say? Would anyone listen?

Last year, over a million people requested the chance to audition for Wheel of Fortune. Fewer than 600 were selected to appear on the show (0.0006 percent).

It's human nature to take a look at those numbers and ask, "What's the point in applying and auditioning for a show that one-million people are vying to be on?"

However, faith looks at those overwhelming odds with a big smile and knows – with God all things are possible.

This *best-selling autobiographical novel* follows a group of ten random 'Wheel of Fortune' fanatics, who met for lunch every weekday to play an online Twitter game, and 50% (5 of 10) became contestants on America's favorite game-show.

More than 800 times greater than the general population. (835) X (0.0006) = 50 percent. This statistic shows the heart of these individuals and exemplifies the words of John A. Passaro, "If your dreams are big enough, then the odds just don't matter."

With the chance of appearing on Wheel of Fortune nearly impossible, the fact that fifty-percent made it on the game-show, allows me to proudly proclaim that the crew saw the odds and not only conquered them, they blew them out of the water!

After finishing our meals, I feel excited, exhilarated, and refreshed. I feel a newfound appreciation for conversation. I feel like my social palette has been thoroughly cleansed.

You see, before I started the Short-bus-Crew by creating a collage using the avatars of ten random Twitter Toss-Up players, God had armed me with a piece of advice.

HE suggested that I come in without any expectations. Too often we head into meet-ups hoping to get something out of the situation. If expectations aren't met, we leave disappointed.

In the case of the Short-bus-Crew, coming without a plan helped unfamiliar faces open up to one another, have meaningful conversations and enjoy the novelty of it all.

Indeed, the very basis of social media interaction, with a new experience formed each and every time.

And if it isn't painfully obvious yet, after 3 final auditions, I am in the fifty-percentile that have not been called for a taping.

Four crew members (5 including Chip's husband, Bruce) received the golden letter from Culver City at the time this book was published and all four made it to the bonus-round winning over two-hundred thousand dollars ($202,059).

---

"Dreams are always crushing when they don't come true. But it's the simple dreams that are often the most painful because they seem so personal, so reasonable, so attainable. You're always close enough to touch, but never quite close enough to hold and it's enough to break your heart."

Nicholas Sparks, *Three Weeks With My Brother*

Carrie Grosvenor, About.com's game-show expert, wrote: "Hey Skinny, you should be encouraged, no matter what happens. Only one percent, roughly 10,000 people out of the one-million who apply get to the final auditions, so making it that far is huge!"

Overachiever than I am, I managed to accomplish that feat 3 times. When it comes to Wheel of Fortune final auditions, I am something of a prodigy.

As I began to see each of my friends appear on TV, on the stage I wanted to stand; talking with Pat, flirting with Vanna, under a shower of confetti like the three, million-dollar winners: (S)arah Manchester, (A)utumn Erhard, (M)ichelle Loewenstein; book cover model (S.A.M.) is a composite image of their faces, one would think that it was only natural for negative thoughts of jealousy and envy to creep in.

Although it varies according to cultures or personalities, the feeling of jealousy is common to all human beings. However, bonds formed with each of these remarkable individuals would not allow for a single negative emotion to fill my body but only feelings of joy. It feels unimaginably good to be happy for others.

*Philippians 4:4-5* says – "Always be full of joy in the Lord; I say it again, rejoice! Let everyone see that you are unselfish and considerate. Let your gentleness be evident to all. And remember that the Lord is coming soon."

As I celebrated and cheered for my crew-mates, I realized not getting the letter didn't stop me from reaching my dream. As a child, I dreamed of becoming a writer, then I grew up. Dreams never die. They niggle at us. They want out – if given the chance.

The best told stories involve vanquishing huge odds and achieving victory. Well, that's Short-bus-Crew – here's the chance.

What inspired this book was serendipity. I found myself sharing lunches with random strangers, clueless to their identities. One day, I decided to say, "What's up!"

During this adventure to make it on Wheel of Fortune, I discovered my God-given-Dream and what it means to have faith. Although the letter hasn't arrived yet, faith is the reason I've hope for the future. Faith allows me to be certain of things to come.

Today, I look past what my eyes can see and focus on the vision that's in my heart. My faith is the difference between simply hoping for something and knowing for certain that it will happen.

You can read about my appearance on Wheel of Fortune in the upcoming sequel – THANK HIM FOR HIS ANSWERS, from New York Times best selling author of - Fill in the Blank.

*Philippians 4:6-7* says — "Don't worry about anything; instead, pray about everything; tell God your needs and don't forget to thank him for his answers. If you do this, you will experience God's peace, which is far more wonderful than the human mind can understand."

"Everything will fall into place, be patient." *Mark Anthony Linton*

# Author's **NOTES**

This work isn't authorized by Wheel of Fortune, CBS Television, Sony or other company-entity associated with Wheel of Fortune. Wheel of Fortune, CBS and Sony companies are all registered trademarks, and this work is not intended to infringe upon any of these trademarks.

Blatt, Ben. "The Hardest Puzzles in Wheel of Fortune History: Where Does New Baby Buggy Rank?" Slate. The Slate Group, 27 Mar. 2014. Web. 1 Jan. 2017.

"Buy a Vowel Boards." N.p., N.d. Web. 1 Jan. 2017.

Carter, Travis. "Reach for the Stars Ministries." Reach for the Stars Ministries. N.p., N.d. Web. 1 Jan. 2017.

Doyle Wille, Kim. Huffington Post. N.p., N.d. Web. 1 Jan. 2017.

Mosher, Chad. ChadMosher.com. N.p., N.d. Web. 1 Jan. 2017.

Webb, Dennis. "Woman's Prior Hardship Served as Fertilizer for Garden Project." The Daily Sentinel. Grand Junction Media, 2 Mar. 2015. Web. 1 Jan. 2017.

# Answer **KEY**

Page 71 (Category: On the Map)

_ _ T _ IN _ _ AM * _ _ G _ A _ _

⚹ NOTTINGHAM ENGLAND


Page 77 (Category: What are you Doing?)

P _ _ _ I _ G * BY * T _ E * R _ LE _

⚹ PLAYING BY THE RULES


Page 78 (Category: Rhyme Time)

I'M * _ OO _ ING * O _ ER * A * _ O _ R - _ EA _ * _ _ O _ ER

⚹ I'M LOOKING OVER A FOUR-LEAF CLOVER


Page 83 (Category: Before & After)

_ ARATE * _ _ O _ * SUE _

⚹ KARATE CHOP SUEY


Page 85 (Category: Movie Quote)

_ _ _ * THE * _ _ R _ E * BE * _ _ TH * _ _ _

⚹ MAY THE FORCE BE WITH YOU

Page 88 (Category: What are you Doing?)

_ _ _ Y _ _ _ * _ _ _ R _ * _ _ _ _ S

✦ PLAYING BOARD GAMES


Page 89 (Category: Event)

ANN _ AL * _ _ _ PAN _ * P _ _ N _ _

✦ ANNUAL COMPANY PICNIC


Page 105 (Category: Character)

_ _ _ _ Y _ * _ H _ * S _ _ _ _ _ * _ _ N

✦ POPEYE THE SAILOR MAN


Page 106 (Category: Food & Drink)

_ E _ N _ _ * B _ T _ _ R * _ A _ _

✦ PEANUT BUTTER BARS

Mark Anthony Linton is a Servant, Father, Realtor, and Author. He's a fan of the Washington Redskins and loves to make people laugh and think. Often one causes the other, both are essential to living. A frequent guest on news programs, he has appeared on ABC's Good Morning America, CBS News, and FOX 5 Atlanta.

———————

CONNECT on Facebook at www.facebook.com/skinnyrealty, on Twitter at @skinnyrealty, and you should send him an email at Mark@LPHbooks.com, if the mood strikes you – GOD bless you.

Made in the USA
Middletown, DE
28 November 2018